Streamlining Your Life

Streamlining Your Life

A 5-point plan for uncomplicated living

Stephanie Culp

Writer's Digest Books

Cincinnati, Ohio

Edited by Beth Franks
Designed by Carol Buchanan

Dedication

For Brittney and Breana Jones

Acknowledgments

Once again, the folks at Writer's Digest Books have provided
steadfast service and patience in working with me on another
project. First I'd like to thank Editorial Director Bill Brohaugh
for getting this idea off the ground. Thanks also go to Mert
Ransdell and Hugh Gildea; both handled critical aspects of my
project with much-appreciated dispatch. In the area of special
sales, Jo Hoff is tops.

Special thanks go to freelance editor Beth Franks, who
pulled out all the stops to help me streamline this book. Her
unique talent and understanding helped shape and reshape the
backbone of the book, and her special touches are found
throughout.

On the home front, as always, Fritz Culp and Jim Reed served
up support, love, and infinite patience—all of which made a
critical difference on a daily basis, thus allowing me to do what
I wanted or needed to do. A new addition, Boca Culp, was by
my side for every minute of the revision process. His presence
definitely enhanced that process, diminishing the irritation factor by at least half.

Thank you all.

Contents

Introduction . . . 1

Streamlining Your Life

We do not do what we want,
and yet we are responsible
for what we are.
Jean-Paul Sartre

As we career full-speed ahead toward the twenty-first century, we seem to be losing control over our personal and professional lives. There isn't enough time to get everything done. Stress mounts daily, keeping up with the status quo becomes impossible, and life is just not what you think it should be. This seemingly never-ending rat race has people yearning for a simpler, more meaningful way of life, and it is for these people that this book is written.

Streamlining can be the answer you've been looking for to change *your* life. Streamlining is a simple process based on a Five-Point Plan:

1. Adjust your attitude.
2. Prioritize and plan goals, obligations and tasks.
3. Eliminate excess.
4. Organize what's important to you.
5. Create systems to help you function better on a daily basis.

If you want to uncomplicate your life, apply these principles. The Five-Point Plan will be explained in detail in coming chapters.

In addition, this book provides dozens of tips and techniques for streamlining specific areas of your life, from effective meetings to simplified shopping; from hassle-free holidays to organized paperwork. *You can put these tips to work for you immediately!*

Some of the advice here has been culled from my other books, which have focused specifically on organizing and systemizing—both key components of the streamlining concept. You'll probably find that many of the tips and techniques overlap into different areas of the Five-Point Plan—and therefore, life. You'll also be reminded of time-honored axioms that have served as good, solid advice for generations. This advice, along with the principles of streamlining, might seem deceptively simple. But they are powerfully effective when practiced consistently.

Whether you want to find a way to play more golf or make love more often, whether you're intent on climbing the corporate ladder, making the social pages, or raising a family, this book will help you find your focus, develop a plan, and streamline your life. Put these ideas to work and you'll find that you have the time and energy you need to make your life whatever you want it to be—today, tomorrow and all the tomorrows after that.

Much Success!

Chapter 1
Streamlining and You

---

*Every cloud has a
silver lining.
Sometimes you just
have to look for it.*

The alarm clock goes off, you pry your eyes open, swing yourself out of bed, and hit the floor running. You work your way—somewhat wildly—through the day, and before you know it, you are falling, exhausted, back into bed. Counting sheep is unnecessary. Instead, you mumble, "There's gotta be a better way" three times before you drop off to sleep, dreaming about all the things you must accomplish tomorrow.

Welcome to Another Day!

The typical day varies, depending on your circumstances. But for the person who never seems to get everything done, and who feels deep down that there *must* be a way to get some real enjoyment out of daily life, the typical day might go like this:

THE WORKING PERSON

The working person gets out of bed, late as usual, and grabs a cup of coffee or a glass of juice, showers, and heads for the closet, where the first obstacle of the day awaits—nothing to wear. The working person pushes past this obstacle and finds *something* to put on, and after a ten-minute search for the keys, races out the door.

At work, things don't get any better. Most working people are convinced that if they didn't have to deal with forty interruptions each day, they could actually get something done. Telephone calls, meetings and people who stop by the desk to chat, eat up five minutes here and ten minutes there. Throw in an unexpected crisis and a major problem regarding miscommunication with a co-worker, and before you know it, the day is nearly gone. All of this chaos did not stop the mail, however; each day brings a mountain of the stuff, adding to the perilous piles of papers that are beginning to surround each working person like a bunker.

Working people often work late trying to catch up (which is impossible), then crawl home exhausted. Doing anything else is out of the question at this point, so they watch a little TV. Some give barely passing attention to their families. For singles, dating during the week is out because they are too tired and cranky to even consider it.

The weekends are not much better. They might do a little work at home, or go into the office on Saturday. Then there are the errands — housework, laundry, yard work and miscellaneous fix-it projects around the house — that are begging for attention. Throw in church and the Sunday paper, and the working person is lucky to be able to sit back long enough to watch a rented video or the football game on TV. On top of all of this, the family demands attention. (If single, friends and family constantly suggest that the working person "get out and meet people," which is the prelude to the dreaded statement: "If you don't hurry up, you'll never get married!") Weekends that should be pleasure-packed become pressure-packed, what with all that needs to be done over the limited two-day period. By Sunday, most working people view Monday's arrival with dread. The weekend has been only slightly better than the weekday. No wonder they call it blue Monday.

THE BUSINESS OWNER

The business owner's day is similar, only much more hectic. Business owners typically work a sixty- to eighty-hour week. Finding the time to pick up the dry cleaning becomes a major challenge. Business owners push more paper, handle more crises and single-handedly plug more business dikes that are about to break than other working people. Hustle is often the business

5

owner's middle name, and the energy required to keep the business going (according to the business owner) is enormous. This leaves no time for anything else. Family life is minimal at best, and hitting the social scene for singles is unthinkable unless there is a sound business reason for it, such as making a new business contact. Some business owners are on a seemingly do-or-die fast track and can't or won't get off—at least not this week. Perhaps next week. Of course, next week turns into this week, and life for business owners and those around them goes on at its usual, frenetic, unstoppable, and unmanageable pace. Eventually, what the business owner has is a business, but no life.

THE WORKING MOTHER

The working mother faces the same obstacles as the working person described earlier, except that her day starts earlier and ends far later. Mom gets up extra early to get the kids out of bed and ready for school or day care. Since kids don't always pop out of bed like toast at the push of a button, sometimes this takes some extra doing. Once up, they need to be fed, dressed and ready to go on time. This is no small feat, but somehow Mom does it, and puts some clothes on her own back as well. The last minute search for keys is intensified, while certain members of the brood add to the panic and confusion by wailing that they can't find their homework, their mittens or their show-and-tell treasure. Eventually, everybody gets off, and Mom gets to work, with several hours of work already under her belt. And her day has just begun.

Mom's day at work mimics that of other working people. Whether she is a secretary or an executive, interruptions, confused communication, demands from bosses and colleagues, and mountains of mail all conspire to ruin what could have been a relatively peaceful and productive day. If she's lucky, she won't get a call from the school demanding that she drop everything and pick up little Johnny, who punched little Ricky when they were on the playground.

6

The end of the workday brings no relief whatsoever. Another working person might be able to collapse on the couch in front of the tube, but Mom is heading into her third shift of the day. The children—from toddlers to teens—have a list of demands that must be met the minute Mom walks in the door. Seemingly, these kids cannot wait another minute to get what they need, whether it is attention or a ride to the mall. Mom tries to fend off the demands as best she can until after dinner. And, of course, she has to prepare dinner, but if she didn't go to the grocery store, she might have to put her coat back on and go back out to get what she needs before she can get down to the business of cooking. After dinner, unless the kids have gradua-ted in age to dish-washing duties, she has to do the dishes. Children who are old enough to do the dishes will do them, but only after Mom has expended more energy nagging than she would have expended to do them herself. Mom might finish the evening with a little paperwork from the office, squeezed in between settling disputes with the kids and supervising home-work efforts, and getting them bathed and to bed. Somewhere in the middle of all of this, she is supposed to offer some loving, understanding attention to her husband, who, let's face it, thinks that his working-person status entitles him to special care and devotion.

Mom gets to bed after everyone else because she has to do a quick load of laundry and iron a few things so everybody can leave the house fully clothed in the morning. Her husband is, of course, already asleep.

THE FULL-TIME MOTHER

The full-time mother doesn't have to deal with the hazards at the workplace like the working mother. Her day, however, starts exactly like the working mother, but once everybody is off to school, the scenario changes significantly. The full-time mother is usually taking care of a baby or two, which means that her constant attention is required so that the little darlings are changed, fed and soothed upon demand. Babies that can crawl or walk must be monitored so that they don't do damage to themselves or to the house. If Mom has older children, chances are they are involved in an assortment of special activities, which means that she has to don her chauffeur's hat nearly every day to drive this one to baseball practice and that one to piano lessons. Mom is the master planner, planning daily trips, birthday parties and family outings. The bigger the family, the more housework and laundry there is—a daily obligation that has to be done in order to keep the place and the people in it clean. Full-time mothers take their job as mothers seriously, and they often enhance it by getting involved in community programs such as the PTA and special charitable and church activities. They have to go to meetings and keep paperwork straight, make phone calls, and work on projects or fundraisers. The mail brings the household bills for processing, along with a mountain of family correspondence to be answered and magazines and catalogs to be read.

Naturally, the full-time mother makes yummy dinners every night, because that's what is expected of her. She works hard, not only because her schedule demands it, but also because full-time mothers are somehow expected to be everything to everybody—perfect, if possible. The sheer effort of trying to match the efficiency and aplomb of archetypal media mothers like Donna Reed or June Cleaver is exhausting in itself. The full-time mother finishes her very long day in much the same manner as the working mother, and just as pooped.

Streamlining as a Solution

Whether you fit one of these descriptions, or whether your situation incorporates bits and pieces of each, chances are you are looking for a solution to your overextended lifestyle. If you are already convinced that there is a better way to get through each day, you are right. By streamlining your life, you can get more out of it. Streamlining might be the answer for you if you find yourself wishing for a better way of life for any of the following reasons:

YOU'VE HAD IT WITH LIFE IN THE FAST LANE. Life in the fast lane is wearing you out. Perhaps you're not as young as you used to be (oh no!); maybe you're just plain tired and can't seem to get rested. Perhaps the reasons for being in the fast lane in the first place have become elusive to you. In any event, life in the fast lane has lost its appeal and you want *out*.

YOU LIKE THE FAST LANE; YOU'D LIKE TO GO FASTER! You're firmly positioned on the fast track, and you're ready to go faster. "Getting ahead" is your middle name. The problem is, you can't seem to go any faster, because every day is littered with the obligatory clutter of life—from interruptions to too many papers and belongings requiring time, attention and care—and you can't seem to find the time or the space you need to gather that extra speed you need to move ahead. You know you're capable, but you seem to be stuck at your current level, and what you really are now is *frustrated*.

YOU'RE SPENDING MORE TIME TAKING CARE OF THE "STUFF" IN YOUR LIFE THAN YOU ARE TAKING CARE OF YOURSELF. You're totally overwhelmed with all of your belongings, from books by the hundreds, to closets stuffed with clothes and cabinets full of papers. You've suddenly realized that all this *stuff* is not helping you get through the day—it's holding you up. You have to spend time organizing it, cleaning it and finding space to store it all. By the time you've done all that, there's no time to enjoy all these things. Half of it is probably never used anyway. Your possessions are choking the progress of every single day, and you want to conquer the clutter once and for all, so that you can experience life free of the daily complications and work that go hand in hand with all that *unnecessary clutter*.

YOU'RE NOT GETTING WHAT YOU WANT OUT OF LIFE. You have stopped just long enough to ascertain that life has taken a turn you are decidedly unhappy with. The more you contemplate your daily routine, the more you try to find a better way. Sometimes this contemplative period is known as mid-life crisis. But this dilemma faces people of all ages, and the result is an increasingly adamant attitude—you are *not* getting what you want out of life, and nothing anybody says can change that. Only you can change your life, and boy, are you ever *ready to do just that*!

YOU'RE TIRED OF JAM-PACKED DAYS WHERE NOTHING SEEMS TO GET DONE. Your action-packed days have you at the end of your rope. You don't have the energy, and you're tired of the anxiety. You feel like a rat on a treadmill, and you want off so you can walk at a normal pace and actually get somewhere so you can *get things done*.

YOUR RELATIONSHIPS LEAVE A LOT TO BE DESIRED. You're surrounded with people who always want something from you. You give, they take. Or perhaps you're hanging onto old friends for old friends' sake, even though you've outgrown them. Your life is full of social obligations that you resent, and putting on that understanding smile all of the time is wearing thin on your now limited patience. On the other side of the coin, your life might be dotted with people you care about, but *their* patience is wearing thin because you never have any time for them. You're too busy to phone, write, or spend time with friends and family, and as a result, you're missing out on the benefits of close relationships. Your friends and family are about to write you off as someone who doesn't care, and, therefore, doesn't deserve *their* time and affection. You're ready to eliminate relationships that have lost their meaning, and improve those relationships that really are important to you.

YOU WANT TO MAKE EACH MOMENT COUNT. You want to—here it comes—stop and smell the roses. Perhaps you're getting older, or your health is not what it once was. Or you may have reevaluated your priorities, and realized that there is more to life than work and other daily obligations and aggravations. Whatever the reason, you're convinced that now is the time to start making each moment count, you just don't know how. But you do know that you are ready to turn your daily *dream* of roses into a daily *reality*.

The person who is streamlined does not generally have to worry overmuch about these issues. A streamlined person who doesn't want to be in the fast lane is not there, and is doing fine, thank you very much. Those streamlined people who are on a fast track and looking to go faster are doing just that — efficiently and energetically. Streamlined people make sure that their days are productive and clutter-free. They know how to make each moment count so that ultimately they can get what they want out of life.

You, too, can greatly reduce your daily frustrations and anxiety, get more accomplished and find the time to enjoy life, simply by incorporating the principles of streamlining into your routine. This book gives you a master plan, with all the tips and techniques you need to streamline your life and keep it that way.

You'll be able to put this plan to work for you in all areas of your life; this book will explain how. To achieve maximum benefits, work with one principle at a time until you have mastered the entire plan. But even if you are only interested in streamlining one area of your life, such as your closets, or your social life, you can take advantage of the tips that cover that area and put them to work for you immediately. The plan on the next page is the cornerstone.

But first, to help you get a jump start on streamlining, you probably need to find more *time* so you really can do what you want to do. Chapter 2 gives you advice on how to free up bits and pieces of time every day. When put together, this can mean you'll have the extra minutes and hours necessary to start changing your life through streamlining.

The Five-Point
Streamlining Plan

I. ADJUST YOUR ATTITUDE
Stop thinking you can't change things.
You *can* change your life, but first you have to
adjust your attitude.

II. PRIORITIZE AND PLAN
Learn to prioritize. Then make it a habit
to prioritize every thing, person and obligation
on an ongoing basis.

III. ELIMINATE
Eliminate all that is unnecessary. Don't complicate
and clutter your life with a hoard of possessions or
meaningless relationships and obligations.

IV. ORGANIZE
Get yourself, your things and your schedule organized.
Then keep it that way, every day.

V. SYSTEMIZE
Incorporate simple, effective systems into your life to
help you process what must be processed on a daily
basis so that you can actually get things done.

Chapter 2
Finding Time

Lives of great men all remind us
We can make our lives sublime
And, departing, leave behind us
Footprints on the sands of time.

Henry Wadsworth Longfellow

S treamlining promises to give you the time you need to do what you really want to do. But in order to get to that point, you might have to make some immediate changes in how you approach and use the time you already have. Ask yourself these time-related questions:

- Do you have time for yourself on a daily basis?
- Do you regularly reap the rewards that come with delegating tasks and projects to others?
- Are you able to use the time you spend on the telephone to accomplish more in a short amount of time?
- Have you eliminated the daily time-wasters in your life?
- Have you minimized all of the interruptions that are likely to occur on any given day?

If you answered *no* to any of these questions, you must be willing to change the way you spend your time.

WHAT YOU MUST BE WILLING TO DO

FIND TIME FOR YOURSELF. Finding time for yourself is a basic goal as well as a benefit of streamlining. But you need not wait until you are completely streamlined to find time for yourself. Indeed, you must now be *willing to find some time for yourself every day—even if it is only a few minutes' worth.*

DELEGATE. Delegating is the solution to a myriad of time management problems. By hanging on to responsibilities and chores that could conceivably be done by someone else, you are only sabotaging what could otherwise be a streamlined life. Therefore, you must be *willing to let go of your fear of losing control and learn to delegate tasks and projects so that you can have more time for yourself.*

USE THE TELEPHONE EFFECTIVELY. The telephone is a tool that, when used properly, can save enormous amounts of time. You must be *willing to learn how to get the most out of your telephone time by turning the telephone into a time-saver rather than a time-waster.*

DON'T WASTE TIME. Nearly everybody wastes some time every day. You must be *willing to give some thought to the time-wasters that invade your day, and then work to eliminate them.*

CUT DOWN ON INTERRUPTIONS. Interruptions often seem like an unpleasant fact of life. Since your life can be what you make of it, you must be *willing to take charge of the interruptions in your daily life and do whatever is necessary to cut down on most of them so your day is as free of interruptions as possible.*

If you are willing to do these things in order to streamline your life, you would be wise to begin by trying to find some time for yourself every day.

How to Find More Time for Yourself Every Day

You are guaranteed to have more time for yourself if you apply the Five Principles of Streamlining to your life on a short- as well as a long-term basis. You can further guarantee more time for yourself every day if you incorporate these tips into your daily routine:

BUDGET AND SCHEDULE YOUR TIME. Treat your time as if it were a budget, and make sure that your budget includes time for yourself, at least every week, and every day if possible. Schedule that time on your calendar (whether it is thirty minutes or three hours) by making an appointment with yourself in writing. Treat that time as you would any confirmed appointment and resist the temptation to change it.

PRIORITIZE. This is a vital step in the streamlining plan. You must learn to prioritize on a daily, as well as a long-term, basis. Not everything and everyone is equally important to your personal well-being, so keep this in mind as you schedule personal time for yourself. Remember, you are as important as anyone else, and time for yourself on a regular basis is going to give your life some much-needed balance. (We'll cover prioritizing in detail in Chapter 4.)

BE SELECTIVE. Spend less time on unimportant social obligations and concentrate on people who really matter to you. You'll probably find yourself with some spare time that you can then spend on a very important person—yourself.

LEARN TO SAY NO. You might be one of those people who says "yes" too often to requests for time from friends, family and associates, only to wind up with no time for yourself. Say "yes" only if you have the time or it is imperative that you become personally involved in the activity. And unless it is an emergency, don't change that appointment with yourself.

QUIET TIME. Ask others (such as family members) to respect your quiet time, and thank them often for that respect and acknowledgment. For example, insist on twenty minutes of personal quiet time when you get home from work and before you tackle domestic chores. It can make all the difference in how you feel and how you react to those around you.

REDUCE YOUR STANDARDS. It takes an inordinate amount of time to do things perfectly, and while you are busy being perfect, you are robbing yourself of time to do what you want to do. Compromise with yourself and relax your standards on how you do things, from work around the house to special projects. You'll find yourself with a bonus of extra time for yourself. After all, ninety minutes saved each week means an extra six hours for you each month.

DELEGATE. Stop doing everything yourself and you'll have more time for yourself. Send out the laundry, hire a gardener or a house cleaner, or have someone help you with your paperwork and filing. It doesn't cost as much as you might think, and you'll be buying the best gift of all—the gift of time.

CONSOLIDATE. Consolidate tasks, and you'll save a bundle of time. Keep a list of errands and try to do those in the same area all at once so you aren't driving all over town or making several trips. If you plan to cook a meatloaf, cook another one at the same time and freeze it; you'll save yourself the time it takes to put together that dish on another evening. In fact, if you freeze several meals in advance, you can save yourself time well into the upcoming weeks. The time consolidation saves you can be yours, to enjoy as you see fit.

UNDERSTAND THE VALUE OF YOUR TIME. Know that each moment of your life, once spent, is gone forever. Live your life with that in mind, and then plan to make each moment count.

Saving Time Through Delegation

One of the quickest and most effective ways to save time and get things done is to delegate. Individual application, regardless of how competent it is, does not produce as much in the same amount of time as teamwork does. So delegating responsibility or portions of a project to people — creating the "team" — can mean better results in less time than if you did it yourself. The more you are able to delegate, the more streamlined your life will be. You need to know *how* to delegate in order to actually do it.

The first step is to stop thinking that if you want something done right, you'll have to do it yourself. This is nonsense. Almost every task can be delegated, and, with a little training, someone else can complete it successfully.

It is also pointless to fall back on the argument that it will take someone else twice as long to do it. This may be true, but only initially. After you have taken the time to train someone, they should be able to work reasonably quickly. And you will have accomplished what was necessary: the job will be done, and you will have more time for yourself to boot.

In order to delegate, you will need to let go of any "things must be perfect" ideas you might have, and embrace instead the thought that "things must get done." Once you have made this minor mental adjustment, you can move on to saving time by delegating.

Think about it. You can hire others and delegate all manner of things that need to get done. For example, you can hire people to do your:

babysitting	laundry
bookkeeping	organizing
errands	projects
gardening	secretarial and paperwork
housekeeping	shopping

Let others do the things that you don't have the time to do or don't really want to do.

HAVE THINGS DELIVERED. If you can afford it, have things delivered, from groceries and dry cleaning to office supplies.

DON'T LET YOUR BUDGET GET IN THE WAY. If you are on a budget but need to get things done, and would like to delegate some light housework, yard work, babysitting, book-keeping, paperwork or errands, don't forget to look for high school students or senior citizens who might want to lend a hand for a reasonable amount of money.

USE THE BUDDY SYSTEM. You can ask a friend to exchange services with you. If you are great at wrapping gifts at holiday time, for example, and she is great at baking, you can wrap and she can bake.

DON'T TIE YOUR SECRETARY'S HANDS. Make sure you let your secretary do all that he or she is capable of doing. For instance, there's no reason why a secretary cannot open all of the mail, sort and screen it. There is a lot of paperwork that you probably never have to see in the first place—it just needs to be filed or routed. Let your secretary screen and handle your calls, and possibly even assist you with an important project. The title of secretary doesn't necessarily limit your secretary to typing and filing.

DELEGATE, DON'T ABDICATE. Delegating does not mean giving up responsibility; you must still follow up to monitor progress, and accept ultimate responsibility for your projects and tasks.

BE CONCISE. When you delegate, give clear, concise instructions, and then make sure you are available for periodic questions and review of progress at various intervals.

BE POSITIVE. Delegate and train through positive reinforcement rather than negative criticism. Thanking people for their efforts and taking the time to comment on their excellent progress or a job well done produces long-term beneficial results. People will be more willing to work for you, and to do the work exactly to your specifications. Never criticize someone without first acknowledging what was done right.

ASK, DON'T TELL. When working with others, remember to request rather than dictate.

DON'T JUDGE OTHERS BY YOUR OWN STANDARDS. In fact, it might be wise not to judge others at all. Judge their work instead, and be realistic about the standards you set for that.

LOOK BEYOND PERSONALITY. Don't be influenced by personality when you delegate. Delegate according to capability, not personality.

ON THE HOME FRONT

If you've got a family, the easiest way to take care of all the household maintenance is to delegate liberally. You can pay your kids to do chores if you must (Erma Bombeck claimed she paid her kids to breathe). But when they're adults, who is going to pay them to pick up their dirty underwear?

MAKING THE TRANSITION. Don't do things *for* your kids, do things *with* them. Gradually, they'll be doing things themselves.

USE THE GOLDEN RULE. Use the Golden Rule of Housework for Families: Except for babies, no one is too young or too male to help with the housework.

EVERYBODY WASHES. Teach your children how to do laundry as soon as they are big enough. If you have three kids and they each only do one load of laundry per week, that's three loads of wash that you don't have to do.

ADJUST YOUR STANDARDS. When delegating to children, expect a long training period. During this time, they might not complete the task very well, but resist the urge to do it over yourself; it will do until they have learned to do it properly.

TAILOR YOUR EXPECTATIONS. Tailor your expectations to fit the abilities of the child. Children do better if you ask them to pick everything up from the floor rather than to clean up the entire room, which can seem overwhelming. (Once the floor is cleaned up, you can ask them to clear the bed, etc.)

SHARE THE LOAD. Don't be afraid to divvy up the chores and responsibilities with your spouse. If your spouse refuses to pitch in, consider going on strike.

Time-Saving Telephone Tips

*The telephone is a good way
to talk to people without having
to buy them a drink.*
Fran Lebowitz

The telephone can either be a time-saver or a time-waster. If you eliminate time-wasting conversations on the telephone and focus instead on saving time by getting things done over the phone, you can streamline your life even more. Take a good look at how you use the phone, along with how you can best put the phone to use.

TACKLE TELEPHONE TAG. You can avoid telephone tag and get something done if you can accept and return phone calls during specific times of the day. Let everyone know what these times are, and eventually, you'll put an end to continuous telephone tag and actually get something done when you discuss projects and actions needed over the phone.

GET DOWN TO BUSINESS. The people you call will get to the point much quicker if you return their calls right before lunch or at the end of the day. At that time, most people will be anxious to get down to business so they can get off the phone and out the door.

MEET BY CONFERENCE CALL. You can avoid spending time traveling to meetings if you meet over the phone by conference call. The phone company can hook you up to a line that will let you talk with several people on the phone at once, and you are only billed the user fees for that conference call at the time you make it. This is far more cost-effective than traveling to and from a meeting, and, in the case of out-of-town travel, picking up meal and hotel expenses as well.

SHOP BY PHONE. Get department store and mail-order catalogs and shop by phone. You'll get a lot of your shopping done in a fraction of the time. This method of getting things done is particularly helpful at holiday time and for other gift-buying occasions.

CALL RATHER THAN WRITE. If you find yourself getting behind in your personal correspondence, use the telephone. You'll be able to say more in less time than you would have if you had taken the time to put it all in a letter.

DO TWO THINGS AT ONCE. If you spend a significant amount of time visiting with friends on the phone, use that time to get other things done while you talk. For example, you can iron, do some mending, straighten a junk or pencil drawer, clean out your wallet or fold the laundry while you talk. A long telephone cord, a cordless phone or a speaker phone will make it possible for you to move around as you chat.

ORGANIZE THE INFORMATION. If you're going to discuss business on the phone, make sure you have all the necessary information close at hand when you make the call so you don't have to stop to find the information after your party is on the line. If you have everything you need at hand, you might also get your business taken care of during one phone call instead of two or three.

Doing Away With Daily Time-Wasters

As if you could kill time without injuring eternity.
Henry David Thoreau

One of the cornerstones of effective time management is to eliminate everyday time-wasters. Time-wasters have a way of creeping up on people, and before you know it, they have been accepted as an inevitable way of daily life. Time-wasters, like pesky insects, can be eliminated. A diligent application of prevention is required when the time-wasters first try to worm their way into your otherwise streamlined life. These tips should help you get your preventive maintenance program under way:

GET UP ON TIME. Stop lollygagging in bed. If you went to bed when you were supposed to the night before, you wouldn't have any reason to waste time in bed in the morning.

WATCH LESS TV. Spend less time in front of the boob tube — particularly if you only turn it on out of habit — and more time doing things you need or want to do. If you reduce your TV time by only five hours a week, you gain almost eleven days a year. Think about that the next time you automatically reach for the "on" button.

CONSOLIDATE YOUR ERRANDS. Stop wasting time with unnecessary trips. Consolidate errands so that you get several done all at once in the same area of town, rather than making lots of separate trips.

DON'T "ANSWER A FEW QUESTIONS." Unless you are applying for a loan, don't waste time filling out questionnaires. Don't allow yourself to get sucked into time-wasting conversations with telephone solicitors and door-to-door salespeople.

"DO IT YOURSELF." Don't spend your time doing things for others that they should do themselves. The next time you feel that automatic "yes" coming to your lips for friend and family demands, stop and ask yourself if that person is capable of doing the task. If *that* answer is yes, *your* answer should be *no*.

AVOID BUSYWORK. If you must get busywork done, get someone else to waste their time doing it for you.

DON'T READ JUNK MAIL. You can open it if you have to, but don't waste even more time reading it.

EDIT YOUR READING. Don't feel obligated to finish an article you have started reading if it turns out to be boring or irrelevant. Chuck it, and save yourself the time you would have otherwise spent being bored by it.

TURN DOWN SOME INVITATIONS. Spend less time with social obligations that do nothing but take up your time. The time you save can be spent with people who really matter to you.

GET A DISHWASHER. Don't you have better things to do than waste your time washing dishes every day?

KISS ICE GOODBYE. If you don't have a self-defrosting refrigerator, get one. Hacking ice out of the inside of the freezer with a chisel is definitely a waste of time in what could otherwise be a perfectly few good hours.

DON'T OVERSTAY YOUR WELCOME. And don't let others overstay their welcome with you. Whether it's a dinner guest or a house guest on your doorstep, or you on theirs, it's up to you to define and enforce the time frame that signals when one has overstayed one's welcome.

24

STOP FUSSING. One of the biggest time-wasters of all is worry. After all, worrying never changed or solved anything.

Reducing Interruptions

There's probably no one who hasn't, at some time or another, been busy all day but accomplished nothing significant. The day starts with the best intentions and plans, but before you know it, it has been haphazardly and chronically interrupted. With each interruption, your distraction increases, and the potential for getting things done and staying on your streamlined course all but disappears. To assess how interruptions impact your day, keep a log, noting the type of interruptions you suffer, and how much time each incident required. (While you're at it, you might want to log how much time *you* spend interrupting others.) Add up the time at the end of the day that has been devoted to interruptions. The figure should give you more than enough motivation to put an end to all but the most critical interruptions. Take that resolve and put it with these tips so that you can regain control over your day and your streamlined life by eliminating interruptions.

BE AN EARLY BIRD. Get into the office at least thirty minutes before everyone else does so that you can have some uninterrupted time to deal with your paperwork and get your priorities set for the day.

TURN YOUR BACK. People are less likely to step into your office if they can't make eye contact, so if you can, place your desk so that you sit with your back to the door. Better yet, *close* the door. To cut down on needless in-person interruptions, keep the door to your office closed.

TAKE A HIKE. If someone drops into your office unexpectedly, immediately stand up. It's a hint that's hard to miss. If necessary, start walking out. Tell the person you were just leaving, and ask if "we can talk as we walk."

WHAT TIME IS IT? If you want to get rid of a visitor who has dropped in and stayed too long, try looking at your watch every few minutes; hopefully he or she will take the hint.

"HAVE A SEAT"—ON THE FLOOR. If you remove extra chairs from the office, people who like to drop by and chat will be less likely to do so, and if they do, they won't stay nearly as long as they would have if they had a chair to sink into.

GOT A MINUTE? If someone stops by or grabs you in the hall and asks you if you have a minute, don't be afraid to say no.

DEALING WITH TELEPHONE CALLS
Telephone interruptions can be maddening. Change your attitude and the way you deal with those interruptions by adopting these few simple techniques:

WHERE IS IT WRITTEN? Just because someone calls you doesn't mean you have to take the call, and just because someone leaves a message doesn't mean you have to return the call. You are the one who should decide whether or not you wish to spend your time with any telephone conversation that is actually nothing more than an interruption.

SCREEN YOUR CALLS. You can screen out unimportant calls in several ways; use an answering machine; use an answering service; have your secretary do it; ask your spouse to do it; and teach your kids how to do it.

DON'T BE A SLAVE TO POLITENESS. Don't let someone take up your time with long-winded conversations just because you are too polite to say that you have other things to do. Politely, but firmly, say that you don't have time to talk right now.

COWARD'S DISCONNECT. Try this when you need to end a phone conversation with someone who is wasting your time: accidentally hang up on yourself. You can blame it on faulty phone equipment.

"HOW CAN I HELP YOU?" When someone interrupts you (either in person or by phone), ask this question right away so that the other person gets right to the point rather than taking up more time than necessary.

MAKE IT A POINT TO GET TO THE POINT. When you take or make a call, announce up front that your time is limited. For example, you can return a call, but keep it short by announcing at the beginning, "I wanted to get back to you, but I only have a couple of minutes. . . How can I help you?"

WE HAVE NO LISTING FOR THAT NAME. If you really want to eliminate telephone interruptions in a meaningful way, change your phone number and get a new unlisted one.

REMEMBER TO SPEND YOUR TIME LIKE MONEY. Carefully

Now that you've taken some immediate steps to find some extra time for yourself, you can begin applying the Five-Point Streamlining Plan to your life. The first step is to adjust your attitude

Chapter 3
Adjust Your Attitude

*The difference
between the impossible
and the possible
lies in your determination.*
Tommy Lasorda

Attitude adjustment is an ongoing process that is directly related to growth. The attitude with which we embark on any new endeavor sets the tone and contributes mightily to the success or failure of that undertaking. Streamlining, as with so much in life, begins with attitude. A bad attitude will sabotage any success you might otherwise enjoy with a streamlined life.

Chances are, you will need to adjust your attitude in one or several areas of your life. Begin by examining your current attitudes to determine which ones stand in the way of your progress. Answer the following questions:

- Deep down, do you like things the way they are; do you *resist change*?
- Are you at the mercy of problems you can't control, and do they seem to plague you with unnerving frequency?
- Do you spend a significant amount of time being annoyed about what people say to you or what you have to say to them?
- Do you have a lot of papers and possessions that you keep because you can't bear to part with them or because you are convinced that you might need them someday?
- Are you convinced that you should do everything perfectly?
- Do you procrastinate on a regular basis?

If you answered *yes* to any of these questions, you must be willing to adjust your attitude regarding those areas of your life before you can get on with the business of streamlining.

> *The basic fact of today*
> *is the tremendous pace of change*
> *in human life.*
> Jawaharlal Nehru

WHAT YOU MUST BE WILLING TO DO

COMMIT TO CHANGE. At the very least, you'll need to make some changes in how you handle your daily obligations and schedule; you might also need to change (or limit) the things you allow to accumulate in your life. To do this, you *must be willing to change.*

SOLVE PROBLEMS. Problems can overturn even the best-laid plans; however, your attitude will determine how effectively you handle them. Problems can control you, sending you into a paralyzing depression, or producing totally nonproductive anxiety—or you can adjust your attitude. A problem, in many respects, is only as big as you allow it to be, so you must be *willing to take control of your problems, rather than letting them control you.*

IMPROVE COMMUNICATION. Communicating with others begins in your head, where the thoughts and attitudes are formed before you speak. Poor attitudes lead to ineffective communication, resulting in interpersonal complications you don't need. Therefore, you must be *willing to recognize the impact of words so those words can contribute to your life rather than complicate it.*

REEVALUATE POSSESSIONS. You must change your attitude about how many belongings you need. Rather than being tied to a world of things, you must be *willing to reevaluate and eliminate some of them by recognizing the true value of everything in your life.*

30

CONTROL PERFECTIONISM. Perfectionism begins with an incorrect attitude about excellence. Striving to achieve perfection is ultimately counterproductive. Therefore, you must be *willing to accept that excellent is not the same as perfect, and adjust your attitude about needing to have everything perfect. Remind yourself that achieving excellence, rather than perfection, is the nobler goal.*

STOP PROCRASTINATING. You must give up your addiction to procrastination, and then be *willing to refuse to give into procrastination in all areas of your life.*

If you are willing to do these things in order to streamline your life, begin by examining your attitude toward change.

Accepting Change

God, give us grace
to accept with serenity
the things that cannot be changed,
courage to change the things
that should be changed,
and the wisdom to distinguish
one from the other.
Reinhold Niebuhr

Streamlining will require some action on your part, and some changes in the way you live. Change is inevitable. It is an exasperating axiom that resisting change generally doesn't *change* anything over the long haul. All it does is put an extra burden on your daily output, since resisting change usually takes more time and effort than accepting it. Evaluate the possibilities that present themselves so you can adapt those changes that will help you streamline your life. Begin with your attitude toward change.

ALWAYS EXPECT THE UNEXPECTED. But make plans anyway. Just factor in some flexibility in scheduling. Things don't always work out the way you'd like, and you'll need a little extra spur-of-the-moment time to deal with those "disasters." On the other hand, opportunities knock when you least expect them, and some flexibility in your thinking and scheduling will let you take advantage of those "delights" that pop up from time to time.

ANTICIPATE CHANGE. Then, when appropriate, don't fight it, embrace it. Things and people change. Jobs come and go, people change and move in and out of your life, and a myriad of other changes are likely to be imposed upon you, whether you like it or not. Change often represents an opportunity to move on to a new, possibly more exciting, period in your life. Think about that when faced with change, and then act accordingly.

MAKE A COMMITMENT TO CHANGE. Rather than waiting for change to sock it to you when you least expect it, why not try to plan for change, or take the first step toward change before it is actually necessary. If you think you might be laid off from work in the near future, what are you waiting for? Get out there and see what the job market is like, *now*, before the ax falls and everybody else is out there knocking on doors with you. Likewise, if you are in a relationship that is not fulfilling, what are you waiting for? Make a change. Withdraw from the relationship now. Time wasted in a bad relationship is time deducted from what could be a good relationship with someone else (or yourself, for that matter).

CHANGE A HABIT THAT IS SLOWING YOU DOWN. Studies show that most habits can be changed in twenty-one days. Therefore, if you commit to changing some aspect of your life today in order to streamline it—and you stick with that commitment for twenty-one days—the chances are excellent that you will have changed for good. Don't tell people you are going to change. Just do it.

Solving Problems

I always view problems as opportunities in work clothes.
Henry Kaiser

Accepting change is one thing; getting past problems is another. Problems can throw a nasty curve into the game of life. Some people are so beset by life's complications that they barely have time to draw a peaceful breath. These poor souls seem to be followed by a black cloud that, with unnerving regularity, dumps horrific, anxiety-producing problems on their heads. They're always in debt, the car keeps breaking down, their relationships are in trouble, they are harassed by their bosses, their kids are rotten, and the family pets die from unknown causes. They don't deserve this, of course—who does? Nevertheless, the cloud makes a streamlined life seem impossible; after all, they're far too busy dealing with all those problems. For others, even occasional problems can muck things up, causing a disruptive blip on the radar screen of their otherwise streamlined life. Some people think that positive thinking is the answer to problems, and others believe in the power of prayer. Prayer can be meaningful at the very least, and miraculous at the very best, and if pasting affirmations on the bathroom or rearview mirror makes a difference in someone's life, so be it. But if you want to cut your problems down to size, and streamline your life so you don't have so many problems to begin with, first try adjusting your attitude about them.

33

CONFRONT ISSUES AND PROBLEMS HEAD-ON. If you avoid them, they'll merely compound, and sooner or later you'll have to deal with them anyway. Problems are always simpler to handle at the beginning. Deal with people who are problems early on. If your best friend begins to take advantage of you, confront your friend, before it becomes a habit. Delayed actions will only prolong the agony and complicate matters.

FACE THE MUSIC. If the problem is yours, admit that you have a problem so you can face it (might as well get that out of the way). Follow up by seeking solutions to your problem and working on it as long as necessary until you've resolved the issue.

Your problem could be as simple as swearing too much, which, with a little diligence, can be corrected. Other problems might call for professional help. Psychological, relationship and behavioral problems can often benefit from counseling, so don't be reluctant to consider seeking such assistance. Areas of weakness can be helped by consultants and teachers as well. If you own a business and can't get the books balanced, get a good bookkeeper and accountant. You can solve your problem and improve your business at the same time.

DON'T WASTE PRECIOUS TIME WORRYING. Worrying about problems is counterproductive and solves nothing. Focus your energies instead on finding the solution—it makes far more sense than fussing and worrying endlessly.

BE PRODUCTIVE. Solve problems, don't make them. Ranting and raving about a problem, getting depressed or focusing on what could have been, what should have been, and "I told you so" is not productive and does not lead to solving the problem itself.

CONCENTRATE ON ONE PROBLEM AT A TIME. It can be difficult, if not impossible, to tackle problems in a piecemeal fashion. Allocate enough time to focus specifically on one prob-

34

lem at a time, then give that problem your complete concentration. The other problems aren't going anywhere while you do this. You can tackle those one at a time as well.

DECIDE TO DECIDE. Postponing decisions will only add to your problems, so decide to decide sooner rather than later. Continued indecisiveness will only turn into a snowball of consequences that can mow you down.

DON'T BE A KNOW-IT-ALL. When solving problems, ask others for advice and answers that will contribute to those solutions. Pretending to know it all is exhausting and pointless, and can make a bad problem much worse.

CUT YOUR LOSSES. If something isn't working and hasn't been working, that situation might be hopeless. "Three strikes and you're out" is a good rule of thumb: when the same problem keeps repeating itself, cut your losses and move on. The sooner you put the problem behind you, the better.

DON'T CRY OVER SPILLED MILK. Alas, the problem-solving process can be fraught with mistakes. No one likes to make mistakes. In spite of this—with the exception of saints—everybody makes them. There's actually a proper attitude about the art of making mistakes:

- Not Guilty. Don't waste your time feeling guilty about mistakes you made or the things that you didn't do and the opportunities that you let pass by.
- A Mistake Is Just Another Way of Doing Things. Try to remember that at all times.
- There's a Lesson In That. Do your best to avoid being stupid twice in the same way. In other words, learn by your mistakes.

Improving Communication

*Although there are
a great many talkers,
few know how to
converse agreeably.*
Judith Martin

Miscommunication with others is guaranteed to complicate even the most sensible lifestyle. Things poorly said, or left unsaid altogether, can create interpersonal problems in every area of your life. We all know that what we say to others is important. Nevertheless, the importance of approaching communication with a positive attitude often gets lost or forgotten in the wake of daily demands and obligations. Countless books have been written on how to communicate, and for every book there are at least ten experts to expound even further on the topic. Those tomes and experts aside, certain basic attitudes will result in more considerate communication between you and yours, as well as all those obnoxious people you have to deal with. This, in turn, should help you reduce those unnecessary people problems and streamline your life.

THINK BEFORE YOU SPEAK. And then think again (yes, again!) before you act. Don't be afraid to speak your mind, but temper it with good manners and a dash of diplomacy. Saying the first thing that pops into your head can be dangerous. This is how people come to say and do unintentionally rude and stupid things. The words you put on paper require thought as well. The next time you write a scathing letter, sit on it a day or two and reread it before you mail it. Chances are you won't mail it at all.

ASSUME NOTHING. Once you start making assumptions about what is going on, you might as well smoke the paranoia pipe. If he wasn't home when you called, for example, you assume he was out on the town. If he was out on the town, he was with another woman. If he was out with another woman, he probably brought her home for a nightcap. If he brought her home for a nightcap. . . . (P.S. His dog got sick and had to be rushed to the vet.)

BE SPECIFIC. While you're at it, never assume that the other person knows what you want. People are not mind readers.

ASK QUESTIONS. If you need information, speak up! If you're not sure what somebody means, ask. You're not a mind reader, either.

ALWAYS CHECK THE FACTS. Just because somebody tells you something doesn't mean it's true. And, unfortunately, you can't always believe what you read, either. So don't be afraid to do a little sleuthing and double-check your "facts" before you act.

PAY ATTENTION. Nobody wants to talk to someone who is daydreaming or whose eyes are wandering around the room to see what else is going on. Force yourself to pay attention.

WATCH YOUR MANNERS. Don't forget to say "please" and "thank you," and a little bit of "sir" and "ma'am" won't hurt, either. Don't get familiar until you are invited to.

DON'T GOSSIP. It will only come back to haunt you, so bite your loose tongue. Loose lips sink ships.

DON'T BE THE JUDGE. Avoid turning your judgmental attitudes into judgmental comments. It is not necessary to point out a fool; fools bring attention to themselves.

DON'T ACCUSE. Don't accuse unless you are in court.

WHEN YOU OPEN YOUR MOUTH, TRY NOT TO PUT YOUR FOOT IN IT. This is often easier said than done. But if you think before you speak, assume nothing and check the facts, chances are you won't say something stupid or insensitive.

ACT, DON'T REACT. This is a variation on the think-before-you-speak theme. Resist the urge to respond (react) immediately to something that you have just heard that you don't like. Think about it first, rather than reacting on impulse. Then respond appropriately so that the issue can be acted upon responsibly.

BE CONSISTENT. Don't change your mind every five minutes. Being erratic does not inspire confidence.

BE TRUSTWORTHY. Keep your promises, and don't make promises you can't keep.

CLARITY COUNTS. So speak clearly. Don't mumble or use slang. Then say what you mean, and mean what you say.

Reevaluating Possessions

We work to become, not to acquire.
Elbert Hubbard

A life overstocked with possessions is not a streamlined life. Before you can effectively eliminate those things you don't need, you might need to adjust your attitude about your possessions.

People accumulate stuff for lots of reasons, from keeping up with the Joneses to compulsive collecting. The fear of letting go is often proportionate to the amount of possessions. Why people invest in more possessions than they need—particularly when those possessions cost money, take up space and require time-consuming upkeep—is a question well worth exploring.

Perhaps you need to examine why you accumulate things before you actually undertake the super streamlining process of eliminating what you don't need and organizing what you do. Try incorporating the following adjustments into your attitude about acquisitions.

NEED IS NOT THE SAME AS WANT. You may *want* that fancy gourmet popcorn popper, but you really don't *need* it. You can still pop popcorn in a pan, like you always have. You might fantasize about a nifty sports car, but you might *need* the serviceable station wagon that is already parked in your garage. Work toward stocking your life with everything you need, rather than choking your life with everything you want.

LEARN TO LET GO. As lives change, needs change, but somehow objects accumulate with no regard for the changed circumstances. (Isn't it about time to let go of college papers from fifteen years ago?) Don't even consider buying things that don't apply to your life today, and let go of other items that merely take up valuable space and return nothing.

FORGET THE JONESES. Stop and think before you buy something just to keep up with the Joneses. The Joneses won't be there to pay the bill when it comes.

DON'T BUY MEMORIES. Stop buying souvenirs—for yourself or for others. What do you need them for? Photographs can remind you of any trip you take.

DON'T BE OBSESSED. Don't have an obsession about your possessions. Remember, you can't take it with you.

An overbundance of things invariably leads to clutter, which can reach daunting proportions. Often the first step to conquering overwhelming clutter is to shift your attitude into first gear with the following attitude adjusters:

OPEN YOUR EYES TO CLUTTER. Stop turning a blind eye to the steady and ever-growing accumulation. Don't wait until the clutter takes over your home or office; at that stage it takes on a life of its own. Resolve to conquer the problem *now* — while you still can.

CLUTTER BE GONE. Regardless of how many possessions you have on hand, remember that clutter, so long as it is not a state of mind, is easily dispensed with.

BEWARE OF THE "BUTS." Watch out for the "buts" as you contemplate an action plan for dealing with your clutter:

"But I might need it someday;
"But I paid good money for this;
"But they don't make things like this anymore."

You'll have to get past all of these belligerent "buts" before you can even begin to conquer the clutter itself. Every time you hear yourself uttering a "but," replace it with a benefit of getting streamlined. Then press on.

Curbing Perfectionism

*There is a difference between
striving for excellence,
and striving for perfection.
The first is attainable, gratifying
and healthy.
The second is unattainable,
frustrating and neurotic.
It is also a terrible waste of time.*
Edwin Bliss

Perfectionists suffer from the mistaken belief that everything in life needs to be perfect — from the color of the walls in their house, to the typeface on their stationery and the way each postage stamp is precisely affixed to all outgoing mail. Persnickety and compulsive, the perfect person can't possibly do anything simply and quickly. Projects — large and small, personal or professional — get put on hold, as the perfect person struggles to find the time to make every little thing just so. While perfectionists work to get everything just so, very little actually gets done, and life starts passing them by. There is no place in the streamlined life for rampant perfectionism; it is a major stumbling block in a truly streamlined life.

Are you a perfectionist and proud of it? If you want to have a streamlined life, you might want to adjust your perfectionist perspective. Here are a few observations and tips for those who are paralyzed by perfectionism:

STOP TRYING TO BE PERFECT. It is a never-ending and time-consuming quest that often results in undone tasks. Doing everything perfectly requires enormous amounts of time, energy and special materials. There's a limit to how much of that is available at any given time.

PERFECT IS NOT THE SAME AS EXCELLENT. Not only that, sometimes (gasp!) even good is good enough.

FUNCTION WITH CREDIBILITY. Functioning efficiently and effectively is not necessarily the same — and is definitely more important — than functioning perfectly. A filing system of some kind is better than no filing system at all (which is due to the fact that you are waiting until you have the time to set the system up perfectly).

BE WILLING TO REDUCE YOUR STANDARDS. The house does not have to be kept perfectly spotless, and you don't need to rewrite a business letter five times to get it "just right."

FOCUS ON THE RESULTS. Keep in mind that results are usually much more important than the method used to achieve those results.

QUIT GIVING IN. Force yourself to stop giving in to perfectionistic tendencies. You'll only overdo. Recognize when enough is enough. Force yourself every day to let at least one imperfect thing happen. And use the "going down for the third time" rule; if you've done something over for the third time, it's time to let it go. Otherwise you'll find yourself drowning in perfectionism.

Overcoming Procrastination

*Make it a point
to do something every day
that you don't want to do.
This is the golden rule
for acquiring the habit of
doing your duty without pain.*
Mark Twain

Everyone procrastinates. A little procrastination here and there won't knock you off your streamlined track. Chronic procrastination is another story. Talk about your bad attitude. Beginning with elaborate excuse-making, hard-core procrastinators always put off until tomorrow what they could do today — because they know they won't do it tomorrow anyway. Eventually, one of these days becomes none of these days, and procrastination turns into a self-destructive set of attitudes guaranteed to get in the way of personal and professional success. R. Alec MacKenzie, author of *The Time Trap*, claims that "procrastination is a close relative of incompetence and a handmaiden of inefficiency." Uh oh. Because streamlining is synonymous with getting things done, procrastination is one mental hurdle that absolutely must be mastered in order to get on with the business of streamlining. Here are some axioms, attitude adjusters and downright tricks to help you get past that old bugaboo, procrastination.

STOP MAKING EXCUSES. Dreaming up excuses for why you haven't done something is tiresome; people soon see through the procrastinator's veil. Your bills don't get paid on time because you don't tend to them on time, not because you didn't get the bills in the first place. Excuses don't fool anyone, so why bother dreaming them up in the first place.

FORGET CREATIVITY. Speaking of excuses, don't use creativity as an excuse to avoid responsibilities. Just because you are an artistic genius (in your own right, of course) doesn't mean that you shouldn't tend to the other, more mundane tasks and daily responsibilities.

HERE COMES THE TRAIN. Use this anonymous quote to motivate you: "Even if you're on the right track, you'll get run over if you just sit there."

DON'T JUST SIT THERE. Doing something is almost always better than doing nothing at all. If a task requires two and a half hours, and you work on it for just thirty minutes a day, the project will be completed in a week. And, if for some reason you can't complete it, at least you will have started on the path to completion.

DO IT BEFORE IT DOES YOU. Procrastination can have a treacherous snowball effect, thus turning it into the beginning of the end. Out-of-control procrastination can turn a simple ticket for a parking violation into a jail sentence.

STOP FUSSING ABOUT WHERE TO START. Just *start*.

SET DANGEROUS DEADLINES. Force your way out of procrastination with critical do-or-die deadlines. For example, if your office is a mess, make an appointment to have an important client stop by next week. You'll be forced to organize your office before the important visit.

FIX THE PLACE UP. Make sure your working environment is pleasant, and that it suits you; also make sure you have needed supplies close at hand. Procrastination often begins in depressing surroundings with inadequate supplies.

USE THE BUDDY SYSTEM. Tell a friend or colleague that you have to finish a project by a certain date, and check in regularly to report your progress. This will help ensure an attitude of commitment rather than procrastination.

DON'T TAKE THE EASY WAY OUT. Cut procrastination short by doing what you must do first, rather than starting with what is easy to do.

DO THE WORST FIRST. If you're faced with cleaning the entire house, and you hate cleaning the bathrooms the most, do them first. The rest of the day will be downhill from there.

INCH BY INCH, IT'S A CINCH. Tackle large projects by working on them in manageable segments. If you tackle a five-hour project by working on it for one hour each day, at the end of one week—voilà!—it will be done.

We cannot do everything at once, but we can do something at once.
Calvin Coolidge

REWARD YOURSELF. Reward yourself regularly for completing all, or part, or a particularly odious task. For example, if you work two hours each day on a ten-hour project, reward yourself at the end of each two-hour period with something relaxing or invigorating. You can take a walk, have a cup of coffee or indulge in some sinful sweets. Or pick up the phone and kill twenty minutes gabbing with a good friend or relative. Whatever. Just incorporate the reward system into your daily routine. It is one of the all-time best weapons against chronic procrastination.

GIVE IT UP. If you keep putting off doing something because it's a chore you hate or don't know how to do, try finding someone else to do it for you. This is called delegating. You may have to pay for it, but don't let that stand in your way. Trust me; try it, you'll like it.

DON'T BE AT THE MERCY OF OTHERS. Set deadlines for others if necessary so you are not at the mercy of *their* procrastination. For example, you can say, "If I don't hear from you by next Friday, I will assume that I can send the report on as is."

BE PERSISTENT. Once you get started, don't give up. Persistence definitely pays. You can push past procrastination and do what your mother always told you to do: *"Finish what you start!"*

Adjusting your attitude really just means getting into the proper state of mind. Once you've done that, you'll be ready to prioritize and plan your streamlined life.

Chapter 4
Prioritize and Plan

The heavens themselves,
the planets,
and this center,
observe degree, priority
and place.
William Shakespeare

Of the five points required in streamlining, this one is probably the most important. As a key component of streamlining, prioritizing and planning must be done faithfully and habitually. Learning to prioritize and plan effectively requires some thought, both for the long and the short term. Give some studied attention to the people, events and obligations in your life so you can assign value accordingly. Since everybody and everything obviously cannot have equal importance, you might have to cut back or eliminate some of those people, events and obligations. This means you might need to rethink your overall priorities before you can truly streamline your life.

To assess your current prioritizing skills, answer these questions:

- Do you have a master life management plan that takes into account your mission in life, your goals, your unfinished business, your projects and your scheduling plans?
- Do you spend time planning which projects you can and will take on, and how you will accomplish them?
- Do you plan your life by taking the time to schedule your day, week and month in advance?
- Do you take time to plan every day before it begins?
- Do you find it easy to say "no" to all the people who make demands on your time and energy?
- Are you spending more time with people you care about, and less time with social obligations that have no meaning for you?

If you answered *no* to any of these questions, you must be willing to reevaluate your priorities and change the way in which you deal with them.

WHAT YOU MUST BE WILLING TO DO

DEVELOP A PRIORITY LIFE MANAGEMENT PLAN. You will need to take the time to carefully consider what you want out of life, and follow up with a plan. You must be *willing to establish your mission and goals, deal with your unfinished business, organize projects that need to be done, and plan and schedule your life on a short- and long-term basis.*

PLAN, PRIORITIZE AND TACKLE PROJECTS. Projects can become overwhelming if they are not well managed. In order to keep a grip on your projects, you must be *willing to plan, prioritize and tackle the projects in your life thoughtfully and responsibly.*

SCHEDULE REGULARLY. Streamlining demands diligent scheduling skills and applications. You must be *willing to plan and prioritize your schedule by the day, week, month and year.*

MAKE PRIORITIZING PART OF YOUR DAILY ROUTINE. It is important to control your daily routine rather than letting it control you. Therefore, you must be *willing to incorporate regular prioritizing techniques into your daily routine to stay on the streamlining track.*

SCREEN PEOPLE. Although it might sound cold-blooded, you must be *willing to accept that not every person is equally important in your life, and prioritize your relationships with that firmly in mind.*

If you are willing to do these things in order to streamline your life, you can begin prioritizing by thinking through and establishing your own Priority Life Management Plan.

The Priority Life Management Plan

(One's) mission is bound by no
preconceived limitations.
It inspires people to
reach for what could be . . .
It aligns personal ambition,
job and organization,
preserves health and family,
and is grounded in . . . values
to equal the basic qualities that used
to be known in less ambiguous days
as character.

Charles Garfield

Prioritizing needs to be incorporated into your daily and long-term plans. If you aren't yet in the habit of planning, and you find prioritizing too esoteric a chore, you might want to reevaluate your outlook on the subject. Remember that people don't plan to fail, but they do plan for success. As the old adage goes, "Fail to plan, plan to fail." To get yourself on the planning and prioritizing fast track, begin by studying your life and the people in it. Decide who and what is meaningful, and which goals are most important to you, and therefore deserve your attention. Then apply the Priority Life Management Plan to your life.

This plan is simple, but powerful. You will be able to write down your mission and your goals, and you'll be able to make a

49

master list of things to do, turning them into projects or scheduled tasks. Finally, you'll be able to schedule your goals, projects and other things that must be done with do-able deadlines onto your calendar. Ultimately, this plan will help you focus your daily priorities so that they can help you get what you really want out of life. All you need is a plain notebook, a pen or pencil, and some quiet time to start applying the plan to your life.

MISSION. Write down your mission in life. This should be a short statement declaring your purpose in life. Ask yourself what you would like for others to say about you after you have died. What would you like to be remembered for? Do you want to be remembered as being a loving, generous soul who helped others? Do you want to be remembered as a creative genius? Do you want to be remembered as a loving parent and pillar of the community? Write it down. For example:

My mission in life is to be loving and generous to my friends and family and those in need, and to provide a moral guidepost for my children to live by and emulate.

GOALS. Goals represent the tangible things we want out of life—from a new car to losing twenty-five pounds to developing more lasting relationships. Force yourself to write down your goals. Make a separate page for each goal, and give each goal a realistic deadline. Have at least one one-year goal, one five-year goal, and one lifetime goal. For each goal, list all of the steps required to make that goal actually happen. Remember that your goals must be realistic and achievable. You must be willing to make necessary sacrifices to achieve your goals.

Remember, too, that statistics show that those people who write their goals down are far more likely to achieve those goals. So write them down! Prioritize your goals by numbering them in order of importance. A goal is just a dream with a deadline.

> *Goals are the basic direction arrows*
> *of your life.*
> Robert Moskowitz

UNFINISHED BUSINESS. This is the supreme to-do list. All the unfinished business swimming around in your head, cluttering up your thoughts, goes on this list. "Pick up the cleaning. Make up with George. Organize the warehouse. Write to Aunt Sophie. Take an exercise class." Write it all down. A commitment on paper leads to a commitment to action, but before you can act, you need to organize and prioritize it all.

PROJECTS. Projects represent your action plan for achieving your goals. Review your mission. Review your goals. Then look at your unfinished business list, and determine your project categories. Possible project categories might include, for example, "Get Organized," "Self-Improvement," "Business Expansion," "Money," "House," and so forth.

Make a page for each of your project categories and then transfer from your unfinished business list all of the "to-do" items that fall into those major project categories. Prioritize each project with a number, and try to never have more than four projects going at a time.

PLANNING AND SCHEDULING. Now it's time to schedule your week, month and day. Planning helps lead us down the road of success—never forget that. Transfer leftover items from your unfinished business list to your calendar (such as "pick up cleaning," which is clearly not a project but an errand). Fill in your daily obligations. Make sure you prioritize and schedule some time for work on your goals or projects, and don't forget that all-important priority—time for yourself! Do this every day, every week and every month. and before you know it, prioritizing and planning will have become a habit.

51

If you want to learn more about establishing your own Priority Life Management Plan and tailoring it to your needs, my book *How to Get Organized When You Don't Have the Time* will help you.

Planning, Prioritizing and Tackling Projects

Since I was twenty-four . . . there
never was any vagueness in my plans
or ideas as to what God's work was
for me.
Florence Nightingale

Projects seem to be an ongoing part of life; you no sooner finish one than you are faced with another. Worse, you can't seem to get one finished before the next begins, and you find yourself facing several projects that need your personal attention. It's unlikely that you will be able to eliminate projects from your life. But you can prioritize and manage the projects you do have, so that your life continues to be as streamlined as you want it to be, even with those projects.

DON'T BITE OFF MORE THAN YOU CAN CHEW. Stop agreeing to take on every project that comes down the pike. Take on only what you can comfortably assimilate into your streamlined life. Learn to assess the pay-back value that goes with projects. If completing a project doesn't contribute to your life, either financially or emotionally, it's not worth taking on in the first place.

FOCUS YOUR ENERGIES ON ONE THING AT A TIME. Even though you might have several projects at any given time, you need to be able to focus your energies for specific periods of uninterrupted time on only one of those projects. If this seems impossible, and you find yourself continuously stressed out by the many demands of multiple projects, perhaps you need to stop and take on only one project at a time.

MAKE YOURSELF UNAVAILABLE. If you have trouble getting projects done, make yourself unavailable to others when you are trying to get important work done. Lock yourself in your office and refuse to see anyone, let your answering machine pick up your calls, or go to a place that has no distractions (such as a cabin in the woods that offers nice scenery, but no people, and no phones).

CHANGE THE WAY YOU DO IT. Don't do things one way just because they've always been done that way. Change how you handle projects so that you can get them done in a streamlined manner. You can use a computer if it is faster, for example, even if it has always been done by hand.

TAKE THE TIME TO DO IT RIGHT THE FIRST TIME. You will save the time you would have otherwise spent redoing a poor job, and it will still be *done*.

KNOW WHEN TO THROW IN THE TOWEL. If you are pursuing a project that is patently pointless, you might be procrastinating—so you don't have to go on to the next project. Don't allow yourself to cloak your procrastination with this type of project persistence; throw in the towel when a project becomes pointless.

DON'T BE OBSESSED BY DETAILS. Don't get caught up in, or sidetracked by, details. Tackle the major components of any project first; fine-tune the details later, if you have time.

FINISH WHAT YOU START. And don't start what you can't finish. Apply this thinking to the projects you consider taking on, and you can eliminate a lot of "undone project" agony before it has a chance to develop. The next time someone asks you to take on a project—even one you think, for some reason, you should—if you know deep down that it is one project too many, *just say no*!

Scheduling and Prioritizing

Scheduling represents an ongoing planning and prioritizing process that is reviewed on a daily basis. Therefore, how you schedule what you do is critical. If your feet hit the floor running in the morning, and you fall into bed exhausted late at night wondering where the day went, you probably aren't planning and prioritizing your schedule to reap the maximum benefits.

Getting things done begins with scheduling them. Rather than making catch-as-catch-can notations on your schedule, you should make entries that are the result of careful thought and effective planning. These tips should help you schedule much more effectively, putting first things first:

START THE NIGHT BEFORE. Prepare your to-do list for tomorrow, tonight.

BE REALISTIC. Don't underestimate the amount of time it will take to complete a project or task. Be realistic, not fantastic.

ALLOCATE YOUR TIME. Include time for work, play, family and spiritual matters, as well as regular time for yourself. A balanced lifestyle is more rewarding and usually lasts longer than an obsessive lifestyle.

USE AN APPOINTMENT BOOK. Get a good appointment book that you feel comfortable with, and make it an integral part of your daily life. It's unrealistic to expect to keep your entire schedule accurately in your head.

KEEP IT HANDY. Keep a calendar or appointment book near the telephone. If you tend to make appointments when you are out, carry one with you as well. Beware of carrying your only master calendar or appointment book with you when you travel.

If it gets lost or stolen, you're in for more than a major headache trying to recreate all those scheduling facts from memory. On the other hand, if you're likely to forget to transfer information to the master calendar (and thus forget or miss something important), you might be better off taking your chances with only one appointment book.

MARK YOUR CALENDAR. Make sure your calendar has adequate space for your handwriting so that you can easily write down appointments and important dates.

FAMILY SCHEDULE. If you must keep track of the schedule for different members in the family, do it on a large wall calendar that everybody can see and use. Once each week, enter upcoming obligations onto the calendar and then insist that everybody check the schedule before they make unreasonable or last-minute demands on others' time and schedules.

INVITATION NOTATION. When you receive interesting invitations — whether it is to a party or to an art gallery opening — make a note of the date on your calendar as soon as you open the invitation. Then put the invitation itself into a special folder so that when you are ready to attend the event, all of the details (such as time and address) can simply be pulled from the file for reference.

KEEP UP WITH CHORES. Schedule time to do the laundry, housework, yardwork and paperwork on a regular basis, rather than letting it pile up.

SCHEDULE THE BILLS. Mark major bill-paying dates on your calendar. For example, you can mark your due dates for health, house and car insurance in advance. This way, large payments won't sneak up and surprise you when you are least prepared to deal with them.

SCHEDULE PROJECTS. Schedule the appropriate amount of time needed to work on projects. If you think a project will take one hour, add thirty minutes for idiot time, since somewhere along the line, some idiot will probably screw things up so that the project takes ninety minutes rather than sixty minutes to complete.

SCHEDULE GOALS. Break long-range goals into manageable short-range segments with deadlines. If achieving a goal is going to take you eighteen months, do something each month to work your way toward achieving that goal.

BE PREPARED. Mark important dates, such as birthdays and anniversaries on your calendar in advance at the beginning of the year.

SCHEDULE DEADLINES. Establish deadlines for getting things done, and then write those deadlines down so that you are reminded of them, and can meet them.

REVIEW YOUR GOALS. Once each week have a planning session with yourself to go over your goals and schedule tasks relating to those goals onto the upcoming week's calendar.

PRIORITIZE PREVENTATIVE MAINTENANCE. Practice good maintenance by scheduling it in advance. Have your car, your house and yourself checked regularly for any problems that are beginning to surface. Then take care of them right away, before they mushroom into major schedule-blasting and time-consuming expensive ordeals.

VOLUNTEER REALISTICALLY. Resist the urge to be a super volunteer. Unless you have unlimited time to spare on your schedule, say no to pleas from others that you help out with "just one more project." Determine how many hours or days a month you can give to volunteer work, schedule that time, and don't be afraid to let people know that you are already booked.

DON'T WAIT. When you make an appointment with the doctor or the dentist, ask for the first appointment of the day so that you don't wind up whiling the day away in the waiting room. If the doctor or dentist still makes you wait an unreasonable amount of time, bill the person for your time.

STICK TO YOUR GUNS. Don't let others (or yourself) upset your schedule with last-minute, unreasonable changes or demands. If someone chronically breaks appointments with you at the last minute, refuse to make further appointments with that person. For those who make last-minute demands that will impact your schedule, a simple, "I'm sorry, I'm busy," will do nicely.

ADJUST TO OTHERS. If others around you have chronically bad scheduling habits, you can either leave them behind (when they can't get ready on time, for example), or adjust your scheduling expectations to accommodate their bad habits. This can mean that you, too, will arrive late, but it might be better than the alternative, which is to drive yourself crazy over their bad habits. The decision is yours, but bear in mind that being crazed does not fit in well with the streamlined life.

PERIODIC REVIEW. Periodically stop and ask yourself if what you are doing at that moment is worthwhile and meaningful to you. If not, drop that activity from your schedule, and move on to the next scheduled task or project.

SAY NO TO SLAVERY. Don't go overboard and be a slave to the clock. Allow some room for personal spontaneity.

RENEGOTIATE. You may have to periodically revise your to-do list in response to changing schedule conditions and priorities. Be prepared to renegotiate your deadlines with yourself at the same time.

MENTAL HEALTH. Take a day off once in a while for no particular reason. Call it a mental health day. Your mental batteries will get a much needed recharge.

PLAN FOR PLEASURE. Then revel in it.

REVIEW YOUR ACCOMPLISHMENTS. At the end of the day, mark off the things you have done (from your to-do list and calendar), and carry over what still needs to be done, if necessary, onto another day on your schedule. But don't get bogged down about what you didn't do; pat yourself on the back for what you *did* do.

COMMIT TO ACTION. Consider your schedule your commitment to action. Goals describe what you want to do, projects break things down into how they should be done, and your schedule reminds you when to do what needs to be done.

BE FLEXIBLE. Unexpected things come up—disasters as well as delights. Leave some room in your schedule to enjoy the good and deal with the bad. Remember, just because there is some white space on your calendar doesn't mean you need to fill it up.

TOMORROW AND TODAY. Plan for tomorrow, but don't worry about it. Take the time to enjoy today before it slips away from you.

Getting Out the Door

There cannot be a crisis next week.
My schedule is already full.
Henry Kissinger

The streamlined life needs to be kick-started every morning so that the day is pleasant, organized and productive. How people handle the start of a new day can have a direct impact on how the day itself will subsequently shape up. Reorganizing and prioritizing your daily routine can help ensure that you do not lose sight of your priorities in the deluge of daily duties. If you want a streamlined day, begin by getting a good head start on it.

GET READY THE NIGHT BEFORE. Decide what you are going to wear the night before, and make sure it is presentable before you go to bed.

GO TO BED. Don't stay up past your bedtime. You'll pay for it tomorrow when you won't want to get out of bed on time.

GET UP. Train yourself to get up thirty minutes earlier and use that as your quiet time to read, write, pamper yourself or indulge in creative thinking. The early bird really does get the worm. Your entire day will be better for this fresher start.

EXERCISE. Start your day by exercising for twenty minutes. You'll have more energy for the rest of the day.

KEEP MAKEUP SIMPLE. You'll save time, money and space in the bathroom.

GET A HAIRCUT THAT'S EASY TO MAINTAIN. You'll spare yourself hours fussing over how your hair looks.

GET TO WORK EARLY. Beat morning traffic by going in early. You'll get the added bonus of extra quiet time in the office before the phones start ringing. If possible, go home early as well so you can beat that traffic pattern and have extra leisure time or time with your family.

COMMUTE WISELY. If you drive, you can listen to educational tapes or books on tape. If you take public transportation, you can listen to tapes with earphones. Commuting on public transportation is also a perfect time to catch up on your reading, correspondence, and projects in progress.

A Day at a Glance: Improving Your Daily Routine

Prioritizing needs to be done habitually. Incorporate the following prioritizing techniques and information into your daily routine:

DAILY PULL. Go through your to-do pile at the beginning of each day, and pull out the priorities for that day, so that important items don't get buried or forgotten.

TO-DO LIST. Keep a to-do list, and check off each item as it is done. This provides a sense of accomplishment and helps you plan and effectively prioritize your schedule.

SET DEADLINES. Establish the time you expect each project or task to take, and stay within that time period. Let others know you are "on deadline" and don't let them distract you or keep you from meeting your self-imposed priority for time allowed to the project.

CONCENTRATE. Concentrate on the matter at hand. Complete one important task before you allow yourself to be distracted by another one.

EVALUATE. Make it a point to continually evaluate your priorities. An errand or the housework is not as important as visiting a friend in the hospital, finishing a report for the boss or spending time with your family.

DON'T GIVE IN. Don't allow yourself to assign high priority to tasks that are the result of inappropriate requests or demands for your time and talent. Inappropriate requests from your spouse, for example, can be declined, negotiated or, in some cases, ignored. Inappropriate demands for your work time from your boss, are, alas, another matter. All of us must suffer occasional time-eating trials and tribulations. Sadly, bosses often create them.

HIGH VS. LOW. Don't even think of beginning work on low-priority items unless high-priority items have been completed.

INFORMATION ANXIETY. Stop thinking you need to know everything, and don't get anxious when you don't have the time to absorb all of the information that comes your way. This attitude results in information anxiety, and as priorities go, there are plenty of other more important things in life to be anxious about without dwelling on this information impossibility.

HARD VS. SMART. Know that working hard is not the same as working smart. Working hard means doing everything by yourself, perfectly. Working smart involves project planning, delegating tasks, taking advantage of new ways of doing things, accepting input from others and giving up standards of perfection for standards of excellence. It's more effective to prioritize and use your time well than to simply work all of the time.

Prioritizing the People in Your Life

*Establishing priorities
and using your time well
aren't things you can pick up
at Harvard Business School.
If you want to make good use
of your time,
you've got to know what's important,
and then give it all you've got.*
Lee Iaccoca

You can combine prioritizing with people skills, and in the process, facilitate better communication and clarify your priorities both at home and at work.

Unless you are a hermit or so obnoxious that no one can stand talking to you, you will deal with people on a regular basis. How you select which relationships to cultivate, and how you handle those relationships that are obligatory can be directly affected by your prioritizing skills. You can put your prioritizing skills to work by taking the time to reevaluate the relationships in your life so that you can allocate your time more justifiably — to spend with the people you *really* care about. These techniques should help you prioritize when dealing with others:

BE REALISTIC. Set realistic expectations for yourself and others. You'll make life a lot easier on yourself. Expecting people to do things for you—whether it's a family member, a friend, or a co-worker—can sometimes be unrealistic. It is best to be prepared to take care of your needs yourself. You will be less likely to allow your expectations of others to become unrealistic. When someone does help you out, consider it one of life's little bonuses.

CLARITY CHECK. Clarify your priorities and those priorities that others set for you (such as your boss). Be prepared to reset or revise those priorities from time to time as conditions in your life change unexpectedly.

ENERGY DRAIN. Just as you have different times of the day when your energy is at a peak, so do others. Remember that, and try to respect and work with others so that everyone gets the maximum productive benefits from their energy patterns, with high-priority items being tackled during high-energy times.

LEARN TO SAY NO. Say it pleasantly but firmly; never defensively. You cannot, nor should you have to, constantly accommodate everyone else's needs at the eventual expense of your own. Avoid adding an excuse, such as "I'm busy" to your no. People who aren't used to hearing you say no will only argue that their need takes priority. A simple, "No, I don't think so," or "No—but thanks for giving me the opportunity to help you," should get your point across.

NOT EVERYONE IS EQUAL. Everyone does not hold equal importance in your life. Some people are more important to you than others. Decide who has priority, and either eliminate spending time with those who don't have meaning, or cut down the time you spend with them so you can spend your time where it counts.

PEOPLE PURGE. Occasionally, it may be necessary to re-evaluate the relationships in your life — from that friend that you have known since your high-school days, to that co-worker you feel obligated to socialize with on holidays. Perhaps it's time to spend less time with the people who don't really matter so that you can spend more time with the people that do. This can be tricky, but it can also be one of the most rewarding aspects of streamlining. Your neighbors, for example, might be a pain in the neck, and you'd love nothing more than to never speak to them again. Wonderful as that prospect sounds, it might not be practical; to-the-death feuds with neighbors have been started over matters even more trifling than a cold shoulder. So keep the lines of communication open, but reduce the number of contacts if you can (don't answer the doorbell every time it rings, for instance). This thinking applies to co-workers as well. Rather than socializing at holiday time, offer a gift and then dash off to your "in-laws." The friend from your high-school days who still thinks like a sixteen-year-old, on the other hand, can be dropped. There is no nice way to drop someone. Telling friends you don't want them in your life is not nice. Keep phone calls brief ("I can't talk, I'm in the middle of something") and don't agree to get together any more ("Sorry, I'm tied up"). There is never any need to explain "middle of something" and "tied up," and anyone who asks should be told that it is a personal matter, followed by a curt, "I really have to go now." Purging people that no longer have meaning in your life is never pleasant, but it is one of those issues that must be confronted to give you the time for people that do count in your life.

BALANCING PEOPLE PRIORITIES. Friendships and relationships should be selected with great care. When they are treated with consideration and respect, they can last a lifetime. And a lifetime might not be long enough if time is used up with inconsequential people. If you find yourself neglecting people who matter to you—such as close friends—because you don't have the time, perhaps you need to reevaluate your priorities so that you can put a little more balance in your life. You might have to force yourself to take the time to meet with those special people; one sure-fire way is to buy tickets to events for yourself and your friends well in advance and book it on your schedule, just as you would any other appointment.

PRIORITY SAMPLER. If you can't find time to be with the family, try thinking of it this way: One of life's highest priorities is parenthood. With this in mind, housework, yard work, and yes, even the football game, should probably take a backseat to the most important duty of all—being a loving member of a family.

Remember, only *you* can take control of your life rather than letting life control you. Prioritizing and planning will help ensure that you achieve that goal.

Chapter 5
Eliminate

Disposal is the handmaiden of an orderly mind.
Norm Crampton

Congratulations! Since you've come this far, you're ready to roll up your sleeves and get to work in the name of streamlining. Now is the time to strip your life of nonessential things, and affirm that you will resist the temptation to gather up a new hoard of possessions. If clutter is a chronic condition in your environment, prepare yourself mentally for the culling process that lies ahead. Look at how you've handled the task in the past, and face up now to the discipline and determination that will be needed to effectively eliminate what you don't need.

To get a fix on which areas of your life could benefit from the elimination process, ask yourself these questions:

- Do you have reasons (excuses) for hanging onto things that you don't use (such as "I might need that someday")?
- Do you have a hard time deciding which possessions to get rid of?
- Do you frequently misplace things and then have a hard time locating them because you are surrounded by clutter?
- Do you find yourself buying things just because they are the latest trend, are on sale, or just because you are trying to keep up with the Joneses?

If you answered *yes* to any of these questions, you must be willing to bite the bullet and get more serious about getting rid of things.

WHAT YOU MUST BE WILLING TO DO

STOP MAKING EXCUSES. Examine your motives for hanging on to things that you don't need or use. Once you have done that, you must be *willing to stop making excuses for keeping those things.*

DECIDE TO DUMP. Things accumulate in large part because people procrastinate, putting off decisions as long as possible (sometimes indefinitely). You must be *willing to stop procrastinating, and decide, once and for all, what needs to be dumped.*

PURGE PAPER. Piles of paper are not productive, and do not contribute to a streamlined life. You must be *willing to purge all unnecessary paper out of your life.*

CONQUER CLUTTER. Belongings accumulate with no regard to one's ever-changing perspective and overall needs. Often those belongings do nothing but clutter up your life. You must be *willing to eliminate the clutter in your life by getting rid of the things that you do not need or use.*

STREAMLINE YOUR SHOPPING. Shopping can all too quickly become a habit that leads to excess. You must be willing to rethink what you "need" to buy and eliminate bad shopping habits that detract from a streamlined life.

If you are willing to do these things in order to streamline your life, begin by eliminating your excuses.

Eliminating Excuses

As you work your way through the elimination process, you will no doubt find yourself making excuses for keeping things. Let's just get that little exercise over with now. Here are your excuses—up front. Chant them if you wish, but then ignore them and get on with your elimination.

I MIGHT NEED IT SOMEDAY. This is like putting a bet down in Las Vegas. You *might* need it someday—then again, you might not. How long have you been playing this hand? If you still haven't needed it, it's time to cash in your chips and walk away from the table.

THERE'S AN ARTICLE I HAVE TO READ IN THAT. There's very little in life that you really *have* to do. Since you obviously *can't* do, see, taste, read or have it all, perhaps you can start accepting that fact by letting go of some of those articles right now.

IT WILL BE WORTH MONEY SOMEDAY. Perhaps, but are you ever going to see that day?

IT WILL COME BACK IN STYLE IF I WAIT LONG ENOUGH. Maybe. But even if it does come back in style, it will be in a slightly different cut and fabric, and you'll never wear it—at least not in public.

IT WAS A GIFT. Remember, it's the thought that counts. So give it as a gift to someone else (like a charity).

I PAID GOOD MONEY FOR IT. Whose fault is that? Don't compound one stupid mistake with another mistake by keeping the first mistake.

AS SOON AS I LOSE TWENTY POUNDS, I'LL BE ABLE TO WEAR IT AGAIN. What a weighty wait. By the time you lose twenty pounds, that rag will probably be totally out of style.

IT'S STILL PERFECTLY GOOD. If it's still so good, how come you never use it?

IT DOESN'T BELONG TO ME, IT BELONGS TO _____.
Then call up _____ and say you are moving the stuff to outside
storage and having the bill sent to its owner. What are you, a
storage company?

I INHERITED IT. Oh. Time to let someone else inherit it
from you, before you die.

IT JUST NEEDS TO BE FIXED AND IT WILL BE GOOD AS
NEW. So fix it. Or dump it.

THEY DON'T MAKE THINGS LIKE THAT ANYMORE.
And for good reason. Nobody in their right mind would have
one. Besides, it doesn't matter how well-made it is if you never
use it.

I'M SAVING IT FOR _____ (fill in that special day
or event that might never happen—like the garage sale you've
been talking about forever). What day or year *do* you really
think this special event will occur? If it's not on your calendar,
it's time to stop saving for that mythical day.

IT WOULD COST A FORTUNE TO REPLACE. If you don't
use it, don't replace it.

IT BRINGS BACK MEMORIES. Old tax returns bring back
memories, too. How many memories do you need to hold in
your hands?

Deciding to Dump

One of the biggest problems with elimination is deciding what
to dump. As you pick up each object, ask yourself the following
questions to help you decide whether or not you should
dump it:

IS IT A DUPLICATE? If it is just like something you already have, *dump it*! Keeping duplicates of things "just in case" is not necessary in the streamlined life.

WHAT IS THE DATE? If it is hopelessly out of date, *dump it*! This includes catalogs from two seasons back, invitations for events long since passed, and price and address lists that have changed.

HOW MUCH WILL IT COST TO STORE IT? Remind yourself constantly that hanging on to things you don't use costs money in storage space and material costs, and can screw up an otherwise streamlined life. If you want more money and a streamlined life, *dump it*!

DO I REALLY HAVE TIME TO READ THIS? Be honest. Do you really have time to read all those trade journals and junk mail? If you're too busy to turn around now, chances are, you'll never get that stuff read. *Dump it*!

DO I USE THIS? Will you really try out that new recipe, or are you just clipping it out of habit so that you can stuff it in the drawer with all of the other lip-smacking, untried recipes? And what about that exercycle that's been gathering dust in the garage for the past five years? If you know you won't use it, get rid of it!

IS QUANTITY MORE IMPORTANT THAN QUALITY? If every available surface is covered with knickknacks, do you really need that quantity? Or could you pull out a selection of the best and go for quality? This goes for all collections, as well as papers—your college papers from ten years ago, children's school papers, personal correspondence, and sales and promotional materials from your business's early years.

DOES SOMEONE ELSE HAVE THIS INFORMATION? If you actually did need this information ten years from now, could you get it from another source, such as the library? If the answer is yes, *dump it*! Why waste space and money storing something you only need once every ten years? Let the library do that for you.

Purging Paper

Americans use fifty million tons of paper annually — which means we consume more than 850 million trees. That means the average American uses about 580 pounds of paper each year.

50 Simple Things You Can Do to
Save the Earth

There's a paper plague upon us that seems to affect nearly every man, woman and child. Look around. If you're not drowning in the daily deluge of paper, chances are you know someone who is. As paper encroaches into daily life, more and more time is spent trying to find it, organize it, act on it and store it so you can find it again when you need it. Streamlining requires that you deal with the plethora of paper once and for all. Hint: A computer will not solve this problem for you; it will probably generate even *more* paper.

If you tend to add papers to your already formidable piles because putting more paper on the pile is easier than trying to figure out what to *do* with it, it's time to purge those papers and stop putting things in piles "just for now." If you don't know where to start, use these guidelines for easy elimination of excess paper:

TRASH IT. Place a *roomy* trash container under your desk or in the area where you open the mail. Then feed the can generously and regularly. Dinky, fancy trash cans have no place in the paper processing area. One day's junk mail alone can topple a boudoir basket.

THAT'S OLD NEWS. Remember that the first four letters of newspapers is n-e-w-s. If you're hanging on to newspapers for days and weeks at a time, you might as well line the birdcage or kitty litter pan with them; they'll serve you best there at that point. Throw newspapers away immediately—better yet, recycle them.

IT'S IN THE MAIL. If you've reached the point where you have mail you haven't opened for days or weeks at a time, you no doubt have wondered what would happen if you just threw it all away and started over tomorrow. Chances are, 80 percent of it would be mailed to you again, and the other 20 percent you wouldn't miss.

"KEEP YOUR JUNK." Tell junk mail solicitors to remove your name from their mailing lists. Toss any junk mail that arrives immediately into the trash without opening it.

INFORMATION OVERLOAD. Limit the number of subscriptions you receive, and review them regularly to make certain you aren't receiving a periodical out of habit, rather than because it provides you with important or interesting information that you have time to enjoy and use.

RECIRCULATE YOUR PUBLICATIONS. If you can't bear to throw magazines away, you can drop them off at the Laundromat or at medical and hospital reception areas.

BE SELECTIVE. Before you read anything, check the table of contents to see if it's worth your time. Then, if possible, clip only what is worth reading, and throw the rest of the periodical away.

DON'T USE A BULLETIN BOARD. It will only become a hanging burial ground for paper clutter.

DON'T GET LIST-HAPPY. Don't have more than one to-do list at any one time.

TRIM THE FAT. Avoid unneeded or excessive recordkeeping that is the result of insecurity and defensive thinking—such as those infamous "CYA" memos.

DON'T STACK YOUR SHOPPING. Don't keep catalogs longer than thirty days, and limit how many you receive. (People with streamlined lives don't spend much time buying things they don't need.)

DON'T KEEP CALENDARS BECAUSE YOU LIKE THE PICTURES. Calendars are for scheduling and planning. Period.

DON'T HANG ON TO EVERY GREETING CARD YOU RECEIVE. This is mindless hoarding that serves no purpose and is anti-streamlining.

BUSINESS CARD BRUTALITY. Just because somebody gives you a business card, doesn't mean you have to keep it. Toss business cards you don't need.

GET RID OF YOUR OLD COLLEGE PAPERS. Who are you still trying to impress?

GET RID OF PAST INFORMATION. Throw out records that are outdated due to changed pricing or address information.

THIS LOOKS GOOD. It might look good, but if you haven't tried a recipe within thirty days after you have clipped it out of the magazine or newspaper, you should throw it away.

DUMP OUTDATED POLICIES AND OWNERSHIP RECORDS. If the IRS says you don't need to keep them, get rid of expired policies and ownership records pertaining to things you no longer own.

CULL YOUR CARTOONS. Stop clipping cartoons, and get rid of at least 50 percent of what you already have. Once you file it, you won't be able to laugh over it.

UPDATE YOUR CHARITY WORK. Get rid of papers relating to previous charity work that has nothing to do with the charity work you are doing now.

DON'T SAVE SALES, BORING, STUPID, OR COVER LETTERS.

DON'T BE SO QUICK. Don't be so quick to throw out financial and past legal papers, and so slow to throw out paper mementos.

THAT'S HISTORY. Get rid of misprinted stationery and rubber stamps that are no longer correct.

ELIMINATE ACCORDION FILES. Things just tend to get lost and forgotten in them.

ELIMINATE PENDING. Pending is just a black hole into which things that you don't quite know what to do with get tossed so that they can get forgotten as soon as possible.

THINK BEFORE YOU FILE. Stop automatically filing so much paper. Remember that 80 percent of everything you file, you never look at again.

PURGE TWICE A YEAR. Go through your files at least twice a year and get rid of useless papers and files. Throw away as much as you can, and move necessary archival legal and financial records to archival or long-term storage.

DON'T BE A COPYCAT. Resist the urge to copy. Every time you use a duplicating machine, you're contributing to the blizzard of papers blanketing the human race.

DON'T FALL FOR THE COMPUTER MYTH. Realize that it is a myth that computers can solve your paper problems. Computers have the capability to generate at least ten times more paper in a day than you ever needed to see in the first place. Computers are nifty—no doubt about it—but don't automatically assume they eliminate piles of papers, because they're likely to do the opposite—create *more* papers.

Conquering Clutter

That which you cannot give away,
you do not possess.
It possesses you.
Ivern Ball

You can eliminate some excess baggage in your life by weeding out your possessions. If you're just storing it, or shuffling it around, if you spend an inordinate amount of time looking after it, cleaning it, or worrying about it, it's time to get serious about eliminating it. Figure out what you pay per square foot for the space that you live in by dividing your monthly rent or mortgage by your total footage of living space. Now look at how much of that space is used to store things you really don't need. Multiply that occupied square footage by your square footage cost. Numbers don't lie. Streamline your life, and invest the money you will save over the next clutter-free, streamlined year. Then watch your money, instead of your clutter, grow.

If you're ready to conquer all of the clutter in your life from A to Z, my book, *How to Conquer Clutter*, can help guide you through the decision making and elimination process.

In the meantime, begin with the Ten Commandments of Clutter shown on the following two pages. Try, too, the following elimination tips and techniques:

The Ten Commandments of Clutter

I. STOP PROCRASTINATING

Stop putting off until tomorrow what you can do
today, especially when you know you probably won't
do it tomorrow anyway. Decide to decide what
you are going to do with the next piece of clutter
that you pick up.

II. QUIT MAKING EXCUSES

Stop making tiresome excuses for your clutter. You
are only fooling yourself, and the clutter is not
going to go away by itself.

III. USE OR LOSE IT

If you're not using it, lose it. Period.

IV. LEARN TO LET GO

As lives change, needs change, but somehow clutter
accumulates with no regard for our changed lives.
Clutter that is merely taking up valuable space and
giving you nothing in return should be tossed or
given away.

V. BE A GIVER

Give things away, right away. Don't wait until you die
to give away china that you don't ever use now. Every
garment that you never wear could be worn by a
less-fortunate person. Friends, relatives and charities
all appreciate a giving person far more than they
do a pack rat.

VI. SET LIMITS

Limit the amount of space you allocate to house your clutter. Closets, bookcases, filing cabinets—all should be limited. Just because one space fills up doesn't mean you should find or buy more space. It means it's time to weed out your clutter to reclaim the space you already have.

VII. USE THE IN-AND-OUT INVENTORY RULE

If something new comes in, something old goes out. Apply this rule to everything from toys to clothes to books and magazines. Stick to it, and you'll always be in control of your clutter.

VIII. LESS IS MORE

The less clutter you have, the more time, money and energy you will have. People will stop nagging you, and you will be under less stress. You will be more productive with a streamlined life.

IX. KEEP EVERYTHING IN ITS PLACE

Find a place for everything, and keep everything in its place. (The blender does not belong in the bedroom, and the mail does not belong in the bathroom.)

X. COMPROMISE

Compromise when you organize your clutter. Don't let perfectionism keep you from doing it or allowing someone else to help you. Functioning efficiently is more important than functioning perfectly. Remember: perfect is not the same as excellent, and sometimes good is good enough.

ELIMINATE NEEDLESS DUPLICATION. Don't keep duplicate appliances, utensils, cosmetics and office supplies that you don't need. Generally speaking, you can only use one thing at a time. Bear this in mind the next time you have to rifle through the utensil drawer past four spatulas or through your desk drawer past twenty pens (half of which have probably dried up, anyway).

MAKE ELIMINATION EASY. Keep a large carton marked "elimination." Then, as you come across things you no longer need or use, put them in the box. Make sure the things in the box are given away at least once each month.

GIVE THINGS AWAY. Right away. Don't let anyone—including yourself—retrieve what has already been tossed or marked for giveaway. Get rid of things immediately, before anyone has time to reconsider.

BITE THE BULLET. Throw things away. Broken, rusty, bug-infested, mildewed, torn or just plain useless items should be tossed without hesitation or remorse into the trash can.

GET IT FIXED. If you have something that is broken, or needs mending, get it fixed so it can be used or worn. Do this *now*.

TURN YOUR TRASH INTO CASH. If you are getting rid of things that have some value, you can either have a garage sale, or you can see if your local resale shop will take the items to sell for you. Really fine things such as antiques and collectibles can be given to an auctioneer to sell for you. Just be reasonable about your financial expections; don't plan on making a killing through any of these venues. Better you should look at it this way: Be happy to have people pay you to haul away the stuff you don't want.

SET LIMITS FOR YOUR KIDS. Teach your children the elimination habit by example. If they're into the hoarding habit, insist on regular elimination sessions, with trips to a charity to get rid of the unwanted or outgrown items. And don't buy your kids new toys unless they get rid of some of the old ones.

SHARE YOUR BOOKS. A book, once read, serves no purpose if it just sits on a shelf for decoration. Keeping hundreds of books that you never look at is *not* impressive, contrary to what you might secretly think. More impressive is the act of passing books on for others to read. You can give your books to libraries, second-hand bookstores, and senior citizens' centers. Look around to find out who could benefit from one of our greatest possessions — books — and pass yours on when you are finished with them.

GIVE BEAUTY AWAY. Don't hang on to heirlooms and beautiful things (such as that silver tea set) that you never use. Give them to friends and family who can use them and who would love to have them.

CUT BACK ON COLLECTING. If you haven't started "collecting" something, don't start now. If you have started, see if you can sell or otherwise dispose of your collection, and stop collecting from that point on. Collection is just another word for more stuff.

NIGHTY-NIGHT. Whatever you do, eliminate unnecessary clutter from the bedroom. This room, above all others, is supposed to provide a restful retreat, and if you have to move stuff to get to the bed, it isn't restful, and it certainly isn't streamlined.

RENT RATHER THAN OWN. You can get rid of cumbersome equipment by renting things you seldom use. For example, if you ski only occasionally, you can rent the equipment. This is probably anti-yuppie, but if you rent, you won't have to fuss trying to find a place to store the equipment when you aren't using it, and you won't have to spend time figuring out how to get it transported to the slopes on the few occasions that you do decide to go skiing.

IT'S IN THE BAG. Stop hoarding paper and plastic bags and gift boxes and ribbons. Streamline that stuff right out of your life.

BYE-BYE BABY. Don't hang on to all of your children's baby things forever. Someone needs them more than you do.

MAP IT OUT. Get rid of maps that you don't use. If you live in New York, you don't need a map of the London underground unless you travel there *regularly*.

GET IN SHAPE. If you're not exercising with your exercise equipment, get rid of it, and get yourself on a walking program that doesn't require any equipment.

HOW CRAFTY. Either finish or get rid of undone craft projects, and give away supplies that you haven't touched in eons.

WALLS OF YELLOW. Don't hang on to every issue of *National Geographic*. Really. You'll only end up with walls lined with bookcases filled with yellow.

MY FEET ARE KILLING ME. Get rid of worn out and unmated socks and stockings with runs in them. And don't think twice about getting rid of shoes that hurt your feet or your back.

ELIMINATE FIRE HAZARDS. Certain storage areas, such as overstuffed closets and the attic, can quickly become a fire hazard. Keep this firmly fixed in your mind, not only as you clean these areas out and eliminate things, but also the next time you are tempted to start stuffing more things into those areas instead of eliminating them in the first place.

THE FINAL FRONTIER. Don't use your garage as a dumping ground for your things. You are only postponing the day of reckoning when this stuff will have to be eliminated anyway.

SERVE NOTICE. Call the people who have been using your garage or basement as a storage unit—and this includes the grown kids. Let them know that the "lease" is up and it is non-renewable. Tell them that they can store their belongings wherever they choose, so long as it's not in your streamlined house or garage. Those away at college or off on a Tibetan retreat can be notified that their belongings will be moved to a self-storage unit nearby. (Don't forget to provide the address of the unit so that your beloved knows where to pay the bill.)

ELIMINATE CAR CLUTTER. Keep a small trash can in the garage to use when you clean out the car. Then clean out the car every few days so the clutter won't get out of control.

NO SALE. Stay away from garage sales unless it's your own. You need to eliminate things, not acquire them.

GIFT EXCHANGE. When you get a gift you don't like, either exchange it immediately or put it directly into your elimination (charity) box for recycling.

NO MORE KNICKKNACKS. Let people know you don't want any more knickknacks for gifts, and get rid of what you already have.

MEMORIES ARE NOT NECESSARILY FOREVER. Eliminate your memorabilia by keeping only a selection of mementos that have serious emotional or financial value.

PHOTO-MANIA. Cull through your photographs and get rid of duplicates, photos of people you don't recognize and poor quality or stupid shots. Then stop taking so many photographs.

DON'T SPREAD CLUTTER. Give gift certificates, tickets to special events and gifts of your time rather than things. Ask that others do the same for you.

DON'T KEEP KEYS. Get rid of mysterious keys that you don't use because you have no idea what they unlock.

TAKE THE DISASTER TEST. If you're having trouble getting rid of the excess in your life, ask yourself what's the worst thing that will happen if you let go of the item. Take the Disaster test. If an earthquake, fire, flood, or other natural disaster were to strike your life tomorrow, could you get by without the item in question?

For example, could you get along without these things?

- Clothes that don't fit
- Old college papers
- Magazines and newspapers
- Knickknacks
- Old cosmetics
- Trophies and plaques from twenty years ago
- Old military uniforms
- Rarely used sports equipment
- Gourmet gadgets
- Stacks of *National Geographic*

Hint: You'd have to.

Streamlined Shopping

Shopping is one task that has to be done on a regular basis whether there's time for it or not. Some shopping can be eliminated altogether, but no matter what you do, you'll still have to go to the grocery store regularly and make periodic forays out to shops and department stores for gifts, school clothes and supplies for the children, new clothes for work or special occasions, and household goods. Streamlining how you approach your shopping can give you more time to do what you really want to do.

SHOPPING DON'TS

DON'T BUY ANYTHING UNLESS YOU HAVE A PLACE TO PUT IT. You'll just wind up with more clutter getting in the way of your streamlined life.

DON'T BUY THINGS JUST BECAUSE THEY ARE ON SALE. If you don't really need something, buying it just because it is on sale is silly.

DON'T BUY CLOTHES THAT DON'T GO WITH ANYTHING. Don't get a fabulous skirt if you don't have at least a couple of tops to wear with it. You'll cram it into your closet and never wear it.

DON'T BUY THINGS JUST TO KEEP UP WITH THE JONESES. The Joneses won't be there to pay the bill when it comes.

DON'T BUY SHOES THAT HURT YOUR FEET. Life is too short to spend it breaking in shoes that *do not* stretch.

DON'T BUY THINGS YOU DON'T NEED. Period.

SHOPPING DO'S

KEEP A LIST. Keep a grocery list in the kitchen, and note items that you need before you run out. This way, you'll always be fully stocked, and you won't have to waste time running to the store at the last minute. At the store, the list will help you keep on track so you don't buy things you don't need. Use lists for other shopping needs as well, from gifts to clothes. Then, when you shop, shop with the list. If it's not on the list, don't buy it!

TAKE ADVANTAGE. Take advantage of off hours, if you can, at restaurants, banks, department stores and the post office. You'll spend less time waiting in line, and receive better service. Avoid shopping when everyone else does (noontime, after work and weekends) if at all possible and you'll save yourself lots of shopping aggravation along with the time.

STRATEGIC PLAN. When you have a day of shopping planned at the mall, start the day by parking your car at the opposite end of where you want to begin your shopping. Walk to the other end to start shopping, and work your way back toward the end of the mall where the car is parked. At the end of the day, when you're dog-tired, you won't have to walk to get to the car.

SHOP AT NIGHT. If you can, do your grocery shopping later at night. Saturday night is perfect for beating the crowds at the supermarket.

PICK YOUR POISON. Shop only in stores that are organized and make sense to you.

SIMPLIFIED COORDINATION. If you need to shop for a garment to go with something you already have, take or wear the item when you go shopping. This way you won't make a mistake with your purchase and have to spend time returning it and looking all over again for what you need.

DOES IT SPEAK ENGLISH? Don't buy anything that has assembly or operational instructions that you can't understand. The frustration you will suffer as a result could throw your streamlined life out of whack and ruin a perfectly good day or two.

GET A GIFT. When you are shopping for yourself, you can pick up a gift as well. If you have children, you'll need children's gifts on hand for those invitations to birthday parties that come up throughout the year (always at the last minute, it seems). You'll also want to keep some generic gifts on hand (such as something to take when invited to a dinner) so that all you have to do is grab the gift and go. By buying gifts throughout the year, you'll either have what you need (in advance) when you need it, or you'll be way ahead of the shopping game when the heavy gift-buying holidays roll around.

INSTANT GIFT. Give a magazine subscription as a gift. All you have to do is order it sent; there's no shopping involved at all.

GIFT OF TIME. If you never have the time to spend with special friends, try ordering theater or concert subscriptions with those friends to ensure that you will see them throughout the year. You can buy the tickets as gifts by simply picking up the phone and ordering the tickets with a credit card.

CONSOLIDATE ERRANDS. It's worth repeating: Consolidate your errands so you don't waste time making several trips when one trip would do.

HIRE AN ERRAND SERVICE. Personalized errand services can do everything for you, from picking up your cleaning to gift buying to grocery shopping. If you don't have the time to do it yourself, hire someone. There are more important things in life than running errands.

USE A PERSONAL SHOPPER. Many shops and department stores have personal shoppers who will help you shop by obtaining the information from you on your preferences and then putting things together for you to look at. They will also call you when new things that they think would suit you come into the store. And you can call your personal shopper and ask them to recommend and select a gift that you need to purchase. They'll make their recommendation, put the purchase on your credit card, wrap it and mail it for you. And all you have to do is make the call to your personal shopper!

CONSIDER THE ENTIRE PRICE. Remember that everything you buy takes up space and requires care; it will need to be organized, stored, washed, dried, ironed, polished and from time to time, maybe even repaired or mended. Therefore, each purchase exacts a price that you pay over and over again in time and storage space. And if you have trouble remembering all of that and still tend to shop too much, remember this: Conspicuous consumption has always been considered tacky, tacky, tacky.

Elimination is more than a process. It is a solution to the problems created by excess in an overcomplicated life.

Chapter 6
Organize

---

*Organizing is what you do
before you do something,
so that when you do it,
it's not all mixed up.*
Christopher Robin in
Winnie the Pooh
by A.A. Milne

Getting and staying organized is a daily duty of the stream-lined life. When things are organized, your access to them, and the efficiency with which you can operate in relation to them, is maximized. Without attention to organization, stream-lining is impossible.

The process of getting organized can be tiresome, and some-times it's helpful to have an expert assist you. But once you have organized your surroundings, it will be easy, even exciting to keep it that way, thus reinforcing your commitment to staying organized well into the future.

To help you take an honest look at what things need to be organized in your life, ask yourself these questions regarding possessions:

- Do you have a closet full of clothes and nothing to wear?
- Is your house a mess most of the time?
- Are things so disorganized that you don't know where to start?

Ask yourself these questions concerning your papers:

- Do you have stacks of reading material—magazines, jour-nals, newspapers and catalogs—that you haven't read for months?
- Do you keep piling up papers and files because your filing cabinets are full and you don't have any place to put them?
- Once you put a piece of paper or file away, do you have trouble finding it again?

If you answered *yes* to any of these questions, you must get down to business and get organized so that you can stay organized and therefore, streamlined, well into the future.

WHAT YOU MUST BE WILLING TO DO

PAPERS. The papers in your life must be organized and kept organized for effective processing on a daily, as well as a long-term basis. Therefore, you must be *willing to organize the paper in your life so that you know where to put a piece of paper when you receive it, and so that you know where to find a piece of paper when you need it.*

POSSESSIONS. Possessions that are necessary or bring pleasure to you need to be organized so that you always have easy access to them. Therefore, you must be *willing to organize everything in your life so that it becomes immediately accessible to you, but does not create clutter in any part of your environment.*

If you are willing to do these things so that you can have a streamlined life and environment, begin by organizing all of the piles of paper in your life.

Organizing Papers

If you have eliminated absolutely all of the paper that you can get rid of, you will need to organize what's left. Paper-pushing need not take over your life; if you organize what you must keep and process on a daily basis, you can move it from here to there and back again with a minimum of aggravation. You'll need to get all of your papers into a central area where they can be organized efficiently for reference, storage or action. Make sure you organize the work area completely; from the top of your desk, to the bookcase shelves that are littered with books and papers. Then, regardless of whether you work out of an office or the kitchen table, you'll have an organized paper-processing center that can be integrated into your streamlined life.

How to organize all of the paper in your life is a complex topic, depending on the types of papers you deal with on a regular basis. For this reason, you may want to follow the detailed plan offered for organizing papers from A to Z in my book *Conquering the Paper Pile-Up*. In the meantime, these tips should help you get the organizing drift.

OPEN THE MAIL FIRST. Don't try to clean up a paper backlog until you've at least handled the paperwork that comes in today's mail. Otherwise, you'll always be dangerously behind the most current matters.

NUMBER PLEASE. Keep all of the business cards and phone numbers that you accumulate on scraps of paper in one place (in a cigar box, for instance). Then, on a regular basis, transfer them to your Rolodex or computerized mailing list. This way you'll never have to dig through everything to find a number before it is entered; you'll only have to look in the cigar box.

CREDIT CARD REGISTRY. Keep an organized list of all of your credit card account numbers in a file. If any of your cards disappear, it will be easier for you to report the loss with pertinent information.

HOW DOES THIS WORK? Keep instructions near equipment. For example, keep the manual for the answering machine underneath it, and keep the instructions for the VCR in the entertainment center under the VCR.

NO TICKY, NO TAKEY. Keep laundry tickets in the car so that you have the tickets with you when you are ready to pick up your laundry. If you don't have a car, keep them in your wallet.

STEP INTO MY OFFICE. If you handle paperwork at home, make sure you have an established work area assigned solely for doing and storing paperwork.

CLEAR THE DECKS. Remember that the top of your desk is a work area, not a storage area. Therefore, get rid of things that are just being stored there, and only have papers that you are actually working on, or are about to work on.

NOTENIK. Resist the urge to add to your disorder by compulsively making notes on dozens of different pieces of paper and notepads.

ORGANIZE AS YOU GO. Organize your paid bills as you go; don't just stuff hundreds of invoices and receipts into a box or large envelope. Eventually you'll have to organize them, and it's much simpler to do it as you go than it is to face a year's worth of disorganized receipts all at once.

USE THE KISS RULE. Set up a filing system using the KISS rule. Keep It Simple, Stupid.

FILE, DON'T PILE. Don't let your filing pile up. Set aside ten to fifteen minutes each day to keep on top of this vital organizational chore.

DAILY DUTY. Once a day, make sure you review the things you have to do and bills you have to pay, to prioritize and organize the work that must get done, no matter what. (Then do it.)

BACK TO BINDERS. Use three-hole binders to store and transport papers. Binders are particularly good for committee reports and minutes, and also can be used for financial records and address lists, which can be divided alphabetically with dividers.

CUSTOM RECIPE BOOK. Organize your clipped recipes in plastic 8½″ × 11″ sheet protectors, by category (desserts, breads, main dishes, etc.) so you can find them and use them. And unless you spend all of your time trying to impress others with your culinary skills, limit your collection of recipes to one binder.

CHECK THE CHILDREN'S PAPERS. Spend a few minutes each evening dealing with the children's paperwork that needs your attention. Don't wait until everyone is racing out the door in the morning to sign field-trip permission slips or absence explanations. By organizing and dealing with these papers the night before, everyone's daily departure will be more organized, and you and your children won't be faced with last-minute you-didn't-sign-it (I-never-saw-it) crises.

SET LIMITS. Limit yourself to a certain amount of space. If your filing cabinet gets full, don't buy another one; clean out the one you have and organize what's in it, and you'll probably have all the room you need.

Organizing Possessions

I did not have three thousand pairs of shoes: I had one thousand and sixty.
Imelda Marcos

Assuming that you have not eliminated everything you own, you'll no doubt still have plenty of *stuff* to live and work with every day. Organizing the space that you live and work in can give you a daily environment that is peaceful and productive. The streamlined person does not walk among clutter and disorder, no siree. By effectively using space and applying good organizational skills on a daily basis, you can hang on to a goodly portion of your stuff and still have a streamlined life. These storage and space organization tips should help you stay organized and streamlined:

A PLACE FOR EVERYTHING. Establish a place for everything, then keep everything in its place. (How many times do you have to hear this?)

CONVENIENCE COUNTS. Make your physical environment at work or at home convenient by having frequently used items readily accessible, even if this means having more than one of the same item (such as scissors, for example, which are used in several rooms).

PARK IT. Have a "parking zone" to put things temporarily when you come in the door. You might also want to think of this as your to-go area, where you can put things that you'll be taking with you when you go out, such as your keys, your purse, and any paperwork that is going with you the next time you leave the house or office.

DO IT ALL ONCE AND FOR ALL. Organize your entire area. Cleaning out a drawer here and there never works. Your entire living or work area should be organized, even if it means you have to hire someone and it takes a week. Otherwise, you'll just find yourself moving your mess around and accomplishing nothing.

CONTAINER STORAGE. Use your imagination along with some creative containers to organize categories of items that you can't live without. Containers that can be adapted to hold all manner of things include clean plastic sweater boxes, the ever-popular cigar box, a sewing basket or box, tool box, tackle box, cash box or artist's supply box, and for smaller items, baby food jars.

DIVIDE YOUR DRAWERS. Use dividers to keep your drawers organized, from your sock drawer to your bathroom drawers. One simple method of dividing a drawer is to put an inexpensive cutlery tray in a drawer; these work particularly well in the drawer that holds small household screws, nuts, bolts and the like, and also in the bathroom.

DON'T BE BOUND BY TRADITION. Don't live by traditional organizational and storage dictates. For example, if you have a home office and need a place to store office supplies, you might consider using an attractive buffet to store them.

HIDDEN STORAGE. Don't forget that you can store things in hidden areas, such as under the bed and behind the couch. However, if you are storing that much stuff, probably you have not eliminated quite as much as you should have, and perhaps a streamlined life is going to be a bit more than you can personally bear.

MAKE YOUR ROOMS DO DOUBLE DUTY. If you only use your dining room on rare formal occasions, you might want to use it the rest of the time as a home office or study area. You can even push the table against the wall (rather than in the center of the room) and put a sleeper sofa against the other wall, thus giving you a place to park an overnight guest.

For more specific ideas on organized storage in every room of your house, you might want to refer to my book *Organized Closets and Storage for Every Room in the House.* From your closet to your bathroom and kitchen cupboards, essential possessions should be stored in an organized manner so that accessing things when you need them is a cinch.

Ten Weekend Projects to Help You Get Organized

Even with the best intentions, you can find yourself facing a schedule that is too crammed and hectic to leave enough time to tackle those undone tasks and still-to-do projects. The result is that you find yourself walking around with a vague sense that you haven't quite got it all "together." To conquer this unfinished feeling, and to start streamlining your life by getting some of those projects done, you might want to set aside some weekends to start or complete the following projects:

1. CLOSET COMMANDO. Clean out and organize all of the closets in your house. Get rid of clothes that are too small or outdated. If you haven't worn it in over a year, you probably

never will, so those items can go as well. If it needs to be mended, send it out or give it to charity. Get rid of shoes that hurt your feet or are outdated. Clean out and organize bathroom, linen and kitchen cabinets as well. Give away, or toss duplicates (you don't need three whisks), or things you never liked and never use (like those purple sheets you got as a gift, but hate). Tackle one closet or cabinet at a time, and work your way systematically through the house until you get it done.

2. FIX IT. Get everything fixed. Gather up everything in the house that needs to be repaired and take it to the appropriate repair facility or call a repair person. Clothes should go to a tailor or seamstress; small appliances need to go to appliance repair shops; jewelry goes to the jeweler; and the clock needs to go to the clock repair shop. Don't waste time repairing things you won't wear or use, and don't try to fix everything yourself. You probably don't have enough time or talent to fix it all, and the time you save will be well worth the money spent for repairs.

3. READ. Go through your bookcase and give away books that you've read and don't need, or have lost interest in. Unless it is a reference book, it can make more sense to pass on a book than to use it as a decoration, letting everyone know how "well-read" you are. Likewise, get rid of all of those backed-up magazines, newspapers, catalogs and journals that are outdated or that you don't have time for, because they've been accumulating for so long. If there is an article you must read, clip it and throw the rest of the periodical away. Then spend the rest of the weekend catching up on the reading that is really important to you. Spend time reading that self-help or business book you've been meaning to get to, then reward yourself by escaping into that romance or spy novel you've been wanting to read for months.

4. PAPER PATROL. Don't wait until tax time to organize your paperwork. Get all of your receipts for the year in order now, and when filing time rolls around, you'll be well ahead of the game. While you're at it, throw out junk mail. Go through

any boxes of papers or files that you have, and purge unnecessary papers there as well. Put what is left in neatly labeled file folders or boxes so that the next time you need a particular piece of paper, you won't have to spend twenty minutes searching for it.

5. INDULGE IN YOUR CREATIVITY. Take a weekend to tackle a craft or other creative project. You can finish that afghan or work on a painting that you've been meaning to get to; try out those new gourmet recipes, or finish that custom woodworking project. Start or complete those creative projects, so that you, and those around you, can enjoy them.

6. SPORTS OVERHAUL. Take time to clean, repair, or service all of your equipment. Get your bike repaired, wax your skis, and pump air into the basketball and volleyball. Check your fishing gear and organize the tackle, and take your tennis racket out to be restrung. Buy any new or extra equipment that you need to update and add to what you already have. The next time a sports opportunity arises, you'll be ready to jump in and take part.

7. CAR CARE. Clean out the trunk and glove compartment, and get the car washed and waxed. Take the car in for servicing, and if you need new tires, get them. After that, regular attention and maintenance in small doses should keep your car and you streamlined and on the go for quite some time.

8. THE FINAL FRONTIER. The garage and basement are often the last outposts for clutter and items that you never use. Start early in the morning and pull everything (yes, everything) out of the basement or garage. Then put back only what you actually need or use. Throw everything else away or give it to charity. If other people are using your garage or basement for storage, call them and tell them to pick up their things before you start. Make sure you dispose of any toxics responsibly, and if you must store mementos in the back of the garage or basement,

repack them in clean uniform boxes with clearly written labels on all sides, and store them on a shelf or in a cabinet.

9. GARAGE SALE. Now that you've cleaned out your closets, cabinets, basement and garage, have a garage sale to get rid of your cast-offs. Price everything to sell—*cheap*! Remember, this is stuff you want to get rid of. At the end of the day, pack up everything that is left over, and take it directly to a charity. Do *not* take it back into the house or garage.

10. HOLIDAY PLANS. It's never too early to get a head start on the holidays,whether it's Thanksgiving or birthdays and anniversaries. Take some time to buy cards, postage and gift wrap. Make a list of gifts, and begin buying some of them. If you'll be entertaining, plan your menus or check with caterers now. If you'll be traveling, firm up your travel plans or outline your itinerary. The holidays and associated activities will be upon you before you know it, and your advance planning can mean the difference between a happy and a harried holiday season. (For more information on streamlining the holidays, see Chapter 8.)

Getting organized is a major commitment that produces bountiful benefits on a daily basis. What are you waiting for?

Chapter 7
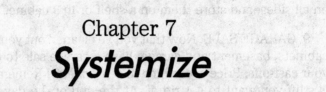
Systemize

---

*If you experience stress,
you're doing it wrong.*

Jay Conrad Levinson

O nce you have organized everything in your life the final step is to put systems in place. While organizing puts everything in order, systemizing helps maintain that order on a daily basis. Systemizing is crucial to a streamlined life; without systems, chaos reigns. Whether you are trying to work your way through the day's mail, or the day's housework, having some simple steps put together into a system for getting things done will be invaluable.

To be effective, systems need to be simple. Devise all of your systems according to the KISS Rule: Keep It Simple, Stupid. Live by that rule, and you'll never resent the systems you have to live by.

Ask yourself these questions so that you can focus on key areas that could stand some systemizing:

- Would you like to file some papers, but don't quite know how or where to file them?
- Do you sometimes put off opening your mail because you aren't prepared to deal with it when it arrives?
- Do you have a hard time keeping your house tidy?
- Are you bogged down with the duties of personal maintenance, such as housework and running errands?
- Does it take you longer to get dressed than it should, only because you can't *find* clothes in your closet?

If you answered *yes* to any of these questions, it's time to implement some systems so your life can sail a smoother course.

WHAT YOU MUST BE WILLING TO DO

PAPER. Papers need to be processed — either by filing them, or acting upon them, or by moving them to another point (hopefully out of your life). This daily demand means that you must be *willing to establish and maintain all the systems required to process, move, and store your papers*.

MAIL. Everyone gets, and is expected to act upon, mail. It rarely arrives at a convenient time. Nevertheless, you must be *willing to establish and follow a daily system for effectively processing your mail*.

HOME FRONT. Most possessions require at least some care and maintenance on a regular basis. You must be *willing to develop simple systems to ensure that your belongings and home are cared for without having that maintenance take over or disrupt your streamlined life*.

SIMPLIFY CLOSET STORAGE. How you look is often directly related to how well-maintained your clothes are in the closets in your home. To be streamlined you must be able to dress well without having to spend time digging through a cluttered closet. You must be *willing to develop a simple system for your clothes storage so that you can always dress in a streamlined manner*.

If you are willing to do these things in the name of a streamlined life, begin by applying these twelve steps to paper management.

Twelve Steps to Lifelong Paper Management

1. OPEN UP. Open and sort the mail as soon as you get it. Throw away all junk inserts, then sort the mail using the four-step paper processing system (which will be explained in a few pages).

2. WORK TO OVERCOME INFORMATION ANXIETY. Stop thinking that you have to be totally informed and aware. Limit the amount of information you try to absorb, and don't feel guilty about information that is beyond your intellectual and time limits.

3. BE REALISTIC ABOUT YOUR READING. Evaluate your subscription list on a regular basis, and if you find yourself falling behind in your reading, let some of those subscriptions lapse. Have someone prescreen business-related reading if you can, and do some screening yourself by clipping only the most important articles for reading and throwing the rest of the periodical away.

4. DECIDE TO DECIDE. Commit to making decisions about your paperwork. Stop putting papers in piles "just for now" because you can't decide what to do with them. Decide to read it, file, pay it or do it. Then *do it*.

5. PRIORITIZE. To ensure that you don't let your to-do box turn into a burial ground, start each day by going through the box and prioritizing what needs to be done. Move these papers to a priority position in the center of your desk. Then deal with those papers first.

6. QUIT PROCRASTINATING. Procrastination is often the beginning of the end. If you find yourself procrastinating on paperwork, try to do the worst first. Or tackle it in small segments—inch by inch, it's a cinch. Or, better yet, delegate it. Let somebody else take care of it for you.

7. STOP BEING A COPYCAT. Resist the urge to copy everything you have on paper. Every time you copy something on a duplicating machine, you're contributing to the blizzard of papers blanketing the human race.

8. STOP DUMPING. Quit using your files as a dumping ground. Remember that 80 percent of everything you file, you never look at again.

9. USE THE KISS RULE. Resist the urge to give in to your perfectionist tendencies by setting up complicated filing systems. Keep It Simple, Stupid.

10. LEARN TO LET GO. Be selective about the papers you keep, particularly where mementos are concerned. Choose a special sampling of paper memories and let the rest of your paper past go.

11. PURGE YOUR PAPERS REGULARLY. Make it a rule to purge your files and papers at least once each year, and more often, if possible. When you have a file out, clean it out.

12. DAILY DUTY. Spend a few minutes each day tidying up your work area and prioritizing your paperwork for the next day. The following day will get off to a much better start if your desk is organized and you are not faced with overwhelming piles of paper.

With these guidelines in mind, let's take a closer look at where most paper originates—with the mail:

Moving the Mail

You may have eliminated a great deal of the paper in your life, and organized the rest of it, but unless you have a system for dealing with the mail on a daily basis, you'll be right back behind the paper eight ball in no time. Before you know it, you'll be using the geologic system of finding papers—you figure if it came in, say, about six months ago, it's about six inches down in one of the piles. You can nip your potential paper pile-up in the bud if you'll implement the four-step paper processing system. Start with today's mail, and use it every day without fail, and you'll be able to maintain your streamlined life without having to hear the growl of that awful paper tiger every day.

FOUR-STEP PAPER PROCESSING SYSTEM

Open the mail as soon as it comes in. Remember, you don't have to act on it that minute, you only have to sort it! You can do it later. There are only four things you can do with a piece of paper! Understand that, and set up four baskets for the following categories:

BASKET #1: This basket is for the things you have to do.
TO DO   You don't have to do it now. You can do it later.

BASKET #2: This basket holds your bills until you pay
TO PAY   them. You will not misplace or forget your due bills as long as you keep them in this basket and review and pay them on a regular basis.

BASKET #3: This one is always a biggie. Again, you'll read
TO READ   it later (uh huh).

BASKET #4: This basket holds all of the papers that are
TO FILE   to be filed. Before you throw stuff in there, take just a minute to remind yourself that 80 percent of everything you file you never look at again.

And, oh yes, you can continue with your elimination habit by throwing stuff in another basket. That's the *trash basket*.

Conquering the Paper Pile-Up

Assuming you handle your mail efficiently every day (don't forget to open it so that you can do this), you'll need to have some other simple systems in place to help move that paper around, and hopefully, out of your life. Everyone's paper circumstances are specific to their particular life, so systems need to be tailored to fit your situation. Entire books have been written about paper systems, and you might want to read one if you're really gung-ho regarding your paperwork, and if you have enough to warrant such research. In the meantime, there are lots of super simple systems you can use to facilitate, bit by bit, moving and organizing that paper, and simultaneously streamlining your life:

GET READY TO READ. Keep a pair of scissors and a stapler in your to-read basket. That way you can clip articles and throw the rest of the magazine away before it ever has a chance to hit the basket.

USE ADDRESS STICKERS. To save time when paying bills, get some inexpensive return address stickers to put on the envelope rather than taking the time to write your return address on every bill envelope.

DON'T DISTURB YOUR BANK STATEMENTS. Rather than separating and distributing the various components of your bank statements (such as separating and filing the canceled checks by category), simply keep the canceled checks, along with the statement, in the envelope they arrived in. Mark the month and year on the front of the envelope and store it in a plastic sweater box on a shelf in a cabinet or a closet. You'll almost never have to refer back to those statements, so why give them valuable drawer or filing cabinet space? You'll save the time you formerly spent sorting, too.

CHECK WITH THE CPA, THE IRS, AND THE LAW. Check with your attorney, your CPA, or the IRS to find out how long you need to keep records; date them with an expiration date before they go into storage, and each year toss the files that have reached the expiration date.

USE PROJECT CARTS. Make use of rolling file carts for special projects. Set up temporary files for the project, organized appropriately. When the project is completed, you can put the files in transfile boxes and store them, thus eliminating unnecessarily clogging current filing cabinets.

READY, SET, GO. Establish a "to-go" area for papers, outgoing mail and files that you need to take with you when you leave. This can be a small table by the door, or a special box on your desk, credenza, or kitchen counter. The closer to the door your to-go box is, the better—so you won't forget to check it when you leave.

KEEP A MASTER FILE FOR EMERGENCIES. Make sure you keep a master file that someone close to you knows about. Include pertinent information that will be needed in case something happens to you, such as the location of your will, ownership documents and bank records, credit card numbers, and insurance policies and other identification certificates and important documents.

---

*Persons without a sense of humor
always write long letters, and
I have noticed, too, that
all madmen write
letters of more than four pages.
I will not venture to assert
that all persons who write
more than four-paged letters
are mad.
Still, the symptom should be
watched.*
Sir Herbert Beerbohm Tree

CHILDREN'S ONE-STOP PAPER SYSTEM. If you're swamped with your children's school papers and art projects, get them each a rolling cart with hanging files on top and oversized baskets on runners under the files. Make hanging files labeled for their reading, writing, spelling, etc., and put manila files inside the hanging files in the cart. Now when the children bring papers home, you can look them over and return them to the children to file in their very own filing system. The oversized art projects will fit in the baskets under the files. Once each year, select only a few of the best papers and store them in a box with the child's name and date on the label. Toss the rest. The cart is now ready for another year of service, and chances are, your child will learn how to keep papers systematically organized—which is something many adults never master.

DROP A LINE. Catch up on your back correspondence. Write letters, notes or cards to all those friends and relatives who complain that you never write. Stock up on stationery, cards, postcards and postage, and put it all in a portable basket. Once you've caught up with the correspondence, you can spend a few minutes each day at breakfast or while you're watching TV to dash off a card so you don't get behind again. Carry postcards and stamps with you so that you can keep up with your correspondence by sending quick notes to people during waiting time spent in reception areas or airports.

If you prefer letters, invest in the time to write one lengthy letter each week to someone who is important to you. At month's end you will have written four lovely letters to four very important people in your life. Or, if you need to correspond with a lot of friends or family, and can't keep up with everyone, every now and then write and photocopy a "newsletter" bringing everyone up to date on your latest antics and accomplishments. If you put a little thought into it, and add a witticism or two, you can send it to dozens of people you'd like to keep in touch with. (If you have a computer, you can use something called "mail merge" to create individualized newsletters for each recipient.)

AT THE OFFICE

Files that aren't set up and maintained properly can be the source of a multitude of paper problems that can add to the anxiety level in your office on a daily basis. The following tips can help you get a handle on your filing system and the papers that are housed within that system.

USE A SIMPLE ALPHABETICAL SYSTEM. When setting up your files, resist the urge to color-code, index or otherwise turn what should be a simple paper storage system into a convoluted nightmare that takes extra time to set up and maintain, requires special supplies and is almost indecipherable without first consulting a file guide or procedure manual.

USE HANGING FILE FOLDERS. It will cost you a bit more money and room, but a hanging file folder permanently marks the spot in the drawer where the file should go. This means, of course, that once the file is removed, it will always be filed in the correct spot when it is returned to the drawer. Eureka! No more misfiles! Hint: You should be able to figure this out, but just in case it has escaped you, you should always put a manila file folder *inside* the hanging folder. This manila folder is what you remove when you need to refer to the file; you never remove the hanging file itself.

USE A TICKLER FILE. Use a tickler file to keep track of orders you may have made—such as orders from catalogs. When the order arrives, throw away the note or catalog page that you put in the file when you placed the order. You're not ordering anything you don't need, are you?

DON'T LET THE FILING PILE UP ON YOU. See to it that you file papers into your system on a regular basis. A filing system is useless if you ignore it and pile instead of file.

DON'T LET MIND-READERS DO YOUR FILING. Circle, highlight or attach a note to your papers to indicate the name and category you want the document(s) filed under. This way, anyone can do your filing for you and mind-readers do not have to be in charge. Not only that, but once it's filed, since *you* picked the title, if, God forbid, you should have to pull the file yourself, you should be able to find it on your own.

BURY DEAD FILES. Store inactive, but necessary, files in transfile boxes, which can then be stored either in off-site storage, in a storeroom, garage or closet. This system for burying dead files leaves you with more space for your daily files and other information that is regularly relevant to your daily paper-pushing routine.

KEEP CROSS-REFERENCING SIMPLE. If you must have a cross-referencing system, a simple "see also" notation written directly on the inside of the file folder jacket should suffice.

TIME-SAVERS BY THE MINUTE

IN EQUALS OUT. Don't let your "in" box become a storage box. Think of it as a "move-it" box, and then deal with those papers every day and make sure you move it!

USE A LETTER OPENER. It helps move things along. Really.

LEARN TO SPEED READ. And carry reading with you to read on the run.

PAPERS ON THE GO. Set up files in your briefcase marked "to do," "to pay," "to file" and "to read," so you can keep your papers organized on the go.

STOP STALLING. Set up a weekly system to recap your business expenses and submit your reimbursement request at that time. Delaying this chore or not organizing it into a system just makes everybody over in the accounting department call you names.

FOLLOW PROCEDURES. If you own a company, or run a department, invest in a procedure manual for your company or department; then keep it updated as procedures change. This way, regardless of who comes or goes, all anybody needs to do is to refer to the procedure manual to understand how to push the paper in your office.

CALL FOR HELP. Don't be afraid to have a professional come in and analyze your paper-pushing methods. A professional can often streamline how you and your company handle paper and save you time and money at the same time.

If you need to know more about what to do with all the papers in your life, my book *Conquering the Paper Pile-Up* will help you decide what to get rid of, how to store the papers you need to keep so that you can find them when you need them, and how to set up systems to help you handle each piece of paper that comes into your life.

Systemizing the Home Front

With my invitations I
Send directions as a guide,
But my house is such a mess
They need a map for the inside.
Phyllis Diller

Assuming that—regardless of your best efforts of elimination—you still have a substantial inventory of belongings, you will need a system for maintaining those things in a streamlined, effective manner. Unfortunately, there are no magic systems for simple daily maintenance. The best you can hope for is to keep one step ahead of it all, so that you don't spend any more time than is absolutely necessary looking after your possessions. Here are a few simple ideas on how to take care of yourself and your belongings. Chances are, you've already heard many of them more than enough times from your loving mother:

KEEP THINGS NEAR THEIR AREA OF USE. For example, pans need to be kept near the stove, and the *TV Guide* should always be kept near the television. Then put things back where they belong. And insist everyone in the house do the same.

EVERYBODY PITCHES IN. If you are a member of a family, insist that each member who is old enough assume responsibility for at least some of their personal maintenance. A toddler can learn to pick up toys and clothes at an early age; an eight-year-old can begin to assume full responsibility for his or her room, and can begin helping in other areas of the house; a teenager can do laundry and yard work; and Dad can do everything that Mom can do. *Everything.*

WRITE IT DOWN. Don't automatically pick up after children and spouses. Write down chores and other obligations so they can't say they didn't know, or forgot what they were supposed to do. Then post the chore list for everybody to see. Also, you can use strategically placed notes to train children to have good organizational habits and systems for their own streamlined lives. For example, a note over their desks can remind them to put papers away, and a note on the closet doors can remind them to put clothes away every day.

USE SUPPORT SERVICES. One of the best methods for handling daily maintenance—from doing laundry and housework to running errands—is to hire someone else to do it for you. You can drop your clothes off at a commercial laundry, you can get a housekeeper to come in once a week to clean, and you can use an errand service to do your errands—from trips to the grocery store to taking the cat to the vet. If you are on a budget, be creative in your search. Cash-starved teenagers and bored seniors can provide a cost-effective labor pool to help you streamline your daily maintenance. Or consider paying your babysitter a bit extra to do some light housework for you.

TAKE THINGS WITH YOU. Consolidate trips. If you have to go down to the basement to get something, take whatever needs to be returned with you when you go. Designate a spot at the top and bottom of the stairs to collect items going up or down the stairs to be put away. Then, whoever is going that way should pick something up and take it along.

DAILY DUTY. Spend at least a few minutes each day in each room of the house at least picking up and putting away any clutter that may have accumulated.

TIDY UP THE NIGHT BEFORE. Each evening, take a few minutes to straighten things up and get your clothes ready for the following day. This way, you won't have to get up to yesterday's mess.

CLEAN BEFORE YOU SIT. Clean off the counters and put pots and pans in the sink to soak before you sit down to eat.

BRUSH, SOAK, CLEAN. Since 75 percent of cleaning is chemical, don't spend so much time and energy scrubbing things. Brush off loose dirt, then soak the item, then clean.

DO IT IN THE NUDE. Try doing the housework naked. Involve your spouse, if you like. It's a new way of doing things that just might put a little joy and amusement into what would otherwise be just an obnoxious chore.

Simple Systems for Your Closets

GROUP YOUR CLOTHES. There are three different ways to organize your clothes closets:

• *Complementary Arrangement.* Put blouses or shirts with complementary skirts or pants. Those things that don't go with anything in your closet should be set aside to be given away.

- *Categorize.* Hang all of your clothes in categories; skirts, pants, blouses, shirts, jackets, suits, dressy clothes, etc. Then mix and match at will.
- *Total Look.* You can hang complete outfits together, such as blouse, skirt and jacket, so that you don't have to rack your brain trying to remember what goes with what, and you can grab an entire ensemble and dress quickly.

COLOR PALETTE. However you group your clothes, you'll want to keep them organized within the groups by color. This helps you coordinate your clothes that much quicker.

INSTALL A NEW SYSTEM. Consider having your closet space "done over," even if you do it yourself. You can often double or triple your space by installing a double-rod system and adding a few more shelves in otherwise wasted space. (For more help organizing your closets, take a look at my book *Organized Closets and Storage*. It takes a room-by-room approach to solving a variety of closet and storage problems.)

You can design your own systems for maintaining your daily life. Systems apply to everything from housework to career planning and managing your leisure time. Be creative and keep it simple, but keep it systemized!

Chapter 8
Streamlining for Special Occasions

---

*Great events
make me quiet and calm;
it is only trifles
that irritate my nerves.*
Queen Victoria

N ot every day is the same, and certain events can do with a special application of streamlining tactics. Life is full of exceptions, and it's those scheduling surprises and other streamlining saboteurs that can threaten to knock you off track. This chapter covers a few of the more common events that are likely to disrupt your life, along with some quick solutions to keep them from getting in your streamlined way.

Hassle-Free Holidays

Before you experience the joy of the holidays, chances are you will run yourself ragged trying to do what needs to be done to make the holidays happen according to tradition. Without eliminating the holiday festivities, you can keep your life stream-lined by making some changes in how you go about getting things done for the holidays:

SET A SHOPPING DEADLINE. Plan your holiday shopping by setting a deadline for completion (prior to the last-minute rush) so you don't get caught up in the last-minute crush at the stores.

TAKE A LIST. Before you do your holiday gift shopping, make a list of who you are buying for, and decide exactly what you are going to buy for each person. Deciding in advance saves you time wasted wandering aimlessly up and down department stores looking for some perfect gift to jump out at you.

NO-SHOPPING GIFTS. The easiest gift of all to give is a gift certificate or tickets to an event. All you have to do is send in an order form or call and place the order with your credit card.

GOURMET GIFTS. Gourmet specialties, home-baked goodies or foods from a special bakery make excellent gifts and don't require a lot of shopping time. If you keep some small gourmet food treats on hand (special jellies, teas or nuts, for instance), you can take them as gifts when you go to parties, or give them as gifts if someone drops by and unexpectedly gives you a gift.

TEEN TREATS. Money is sometimes the best gift for teenagers. Chances are they will be much happier shopping for themselves than if you had tried (usually in vain) to find something they would like.

DRAW NAMES. Why not ask family members to draw names and buy only one or two gifts this year? It will make things easier on everybody.

REVERSE TRADITION. The tradition of buying gifts may be one that you can't keep up with for financial or other reasons. This holiday, try reversing tradition by not giving in to the pressure to purchase so many things. Tell others of your pared down gift list, and ask them to not buy for you as well. Chances are, they'll be as relieved as you are to save time and money.

ORDER IT SHIPPED. To simplify the gift-giving process for friends and family who live out of the area, order those gifts from a catalog. The catalog company will ship—and, in some cases, gift wrap—the gift for you. All you have to do is place and pay for the order.

USE EXPRESS MAIL. If you procrastinate about sending packages at holiday time, you can make use of courier mail services that will (in some cases) even pick it up from your location. Of course, you will pay dearly for this procrastination, since courier mail services are substantially more expensive than services offered by the post office.

WRAP CENTER. If you keep gift wrap on hand, set up a "gift wrap center" in your utility room or in a spare closet or corner. You can make it efficient by installing a round towel rack that can be used to hold rolls of ribbon. Simply cut off what you need when you need it, and spare yourself the aggravation of digging through a box of tangled gift ribbon. Stand up rolls of gift wrap in a small wastebasket, and store flat gift wrap on a shelf or a table under the ribbon rack. Keep a pair of scissors and a roll of tape on a peg for easy access to gift wrap materials year-round. Wrap each gift as soon as you bring it in the door.

ELIMINATE GIFT WRAP ALTOGETHER. If you want to do away with the fuss and storage of gift wrap, use the comic pages of the newspapers to wrap gifts.

MAKE ROOM FOR THE NEW. When new gifts come in, take the time to apply the in-and-out inventory rule (something new comes in, something old goes out). This is particularly good for children who get oodles of presents. Let them sort through their old toys and pull out what they don't want (along with the broken toys) and make a trip to the nearest charity collection center. This automatic weeding out process will make room for the new items, and teach the children some lessons about charitable giving at the same time.

RETURNING RETURNS. If you need to return a gift, first check to see if it is something the store will have in stock after the first of the year. Resist the temptation to return or exchange items the day after Christmas, which is one of the department stores' busiest days of the year.

COPING WITH CARDS. If you need to send out a lot of cards at holiday time, but don't seem to have the time to get them out, you can spend twenty minutes each day on the project, and before you know it, they will be in the mail.

116

ORDER STAMPS BY MAIL. You'll save yourself the agony of standing in line at the post office. Ask your postmaster to send you an order form. Or use your VISA or MasterCard to order stamps. Call (800)782-6724.

UPDATE YOUR CARD LIST. Gather up all of the cards that you received this year and use them to update your card list. Make a small red check on your Rolodex or address book by the name of everyone you wish to send a card to when the holidays roll around again. At the same time, you can add new names as necessary and update your address information. (Remember to put the red check next to any new names you add.) When the holidays come around again, you can simply flip through the list and address cards to all the names you checked. This also makes it simple for someone else to do your envelope addressing if you find yourself short of time next year.

PUT THE TEAM TO WORK. Make the entire family pitch in to help with the holiday chores. You can assign three or more chores to each family member, which adds up to three less things per family member that you have to do.

DELEGATE. If you can, hire others, or pay a teenager to do the major cleaning that needs to be done before company arrives. Your time is better spent doing the other things that make holidays special for your family and friends.

EASY GET-TOGETHER. Rather than putting a lot of work into a major dinner or party, you might want to host a brunch/open house or a dessert and tea get-together.

POT LUCK. If the holiday feast is scheduled at your house, it really isn't necessary that you do all of the cooking. When guests offer to bring something, let them! And if they don't offer, ask them if they would like to bring their "specialty." Most people will be flattered, and will happily do just that.

CLEAN-UP HELP. When dinner guests come into the kitchen to help with the cleanup, don't turn them down. The kitchen is often a great place to congregate and talk while the food is being prepared, and while the dishes are being washed and put away.

YOU'VE GOT TO HAVE FRIENDS. The period between Christmas and the New Year is a good time to call and visit friends and relatives that you haven't had time to see or talk to during the year. Many people have extra time off from work, and now is the time to take in a movie with someone, make a few calls to friends that you are in danger of losing touch with, and to take the time to sit down and send out your personal thoughts and thank-yous to the people who matter the most to you.

GIVE NOTICE. Taking the tree down is never as much fun as putting it up. To make matters worse, it seems that rounding up household volunteers for dismantling it and packing the decorations becomes almost impossible. To avoid nagging the troops, announce the day and time when everything is going to be dismantled, and give notice that you want all hands on deck. Make this chore more fun by turning it into a family party.

TAKE FIVE. Finally, take five minutes out of each day of the holiday season to reflect on the true joys of the holiday season. If you've taken the time in advance to streamline your apporach to the holidays, they should be hassle-free, and you really have the time to make your holiday season jolly.

Streamlined Travel

Being an airline passenger is the opposite of sex: Even when it's good, it's bad.

George Albert Brown

If you want or need to travel, you can spend less time with the fuss and aggravation that's invariably involved with traveling, and more time on the reason for the trip, whether that reason is for business or pleasure. Although it is difficult to fight the transportation gods when it comes to travel, it is possible to streamline your travel so that it is as productive and pleasurable as possible.

PLAN AHEAD. If possible, plan trips well in advance, and if you can avoid it, don't travel during peak holiday times.

DON'T GO UNLESS IT'S NECESSARY. Don't undertake travel for business reasons unless it is absolutely necessary. You'll save lots of time, money and energy if the business objective can be accomplished through conference calls or meetings at a centralized location. If that's not possible, consider sending someone else in your place so that you can continue to maximize the use of your time where it is more productive—at home rather than on the road.

USE A TRAVEL AGENT. You'll save time, aggravation and maybe even some money.

PICK YOUR SEAT. Try to get your seat assignment in advance, through your travel agent. Then have your agent mail you the tickets, complete with the boarding passes. You'll be able to proceed directly to the gate when you get to the airport. (The skycap can check your bags.)

KEEP YOUR TICKETS IN A SAFE PLACE. And keep them in the same place all the time. Your chances of losing or forgetting them will be reduced.

EXPECT DELAYS. When making your travel arrangements, allow plenty of time for unexpected delays. Don't book connecting flights too closely, and try to avoid traveling to and from airports during the rush hour. Get to the airport well in advance so that you can check your bags (if necessary), go through security and check in at the gate without being in a panic.

TIP THE SKYCAP. Tip the skycap at the airport a dollar or two to check your bags. It's well worth the money in terms of time saved that you would have had to spend in line inside the terminal waiting to check your bags at the counter.

DON'T JUST STAND THERE. If you check your bags, and are renting a car at your destination, you can handle the paperwork for the car rental while you are waiting for your baggage to arrive on the carrousel.

SIT FAR FORWARD. Sit as far forward on the airplane as possible so that you are first off the plane and can avoid the crush that invariably occurs in the aisles of the plane as people clog things up trying to collect their hand luggage and move toward the door. If you can't get a forward seat, remain in your seat a few extra minutes (you can read) until the crush begins to dissipate. After all, it's a good bet that your luggage—if you checked it—won't beat you off the plane.

RENTAL RETURN. When you return a car rental, make sure you allow extra time to complete the final paperwork, and to be transported from the car rental depot to the airline departure point.

USE THE TELEPHONE. Travel with a telephone credit card so you can conduct business over the phone during waiting time in airports.

TRAVEL WITH AN ITINERARY. Write up a clear, detailed itinerary, and travel with it as your schedule during that time. Make sure you leave a copy with your secretary, a family member or a neighbor.

PICK YOUR HOTEL CAREFULLY. Try to stay at a hotel that has business services available, such as access to a copier, fax machine and overnight mail services. With this equipment, you can generate a day's worth of work to be completed by your secretary back at the office, even though you are not there.

LET THE CONCIERGE BE YOUR HOST. Have the hotel concierge make reservations and recommendations for you for dinner and the theatre, for example.

PRE-PACK. If you travel frequently, keep a travel kit packed with toiletries ready to go. When you pack, you'll only have to grab the kit rather than rummage around in the bathroom trying to pull everything together at the last minute. A good way to stock the kit is with the sample-sized toiletries that you get in some hotel rooms or can buy in the grocery or drugstore. They take up minimal space and are less likely to leak than larger bottles. Keep a spare toothbrush and razor in the kit, and when you travel, you don't even have to think about it. Just grab the bag and go.

TRAVEL LIGHT. The more you pack, the more you have to lug around, and the more you have to launder or dry clean when you return. Figure out what you need to take and then take half of that.

TAKE AN EXTRA BAG. If you think you'll come back with more than you take, pack an extra soft nylon suitcase or large bag inside your suitcase so you can pack it with the extra items to bring back with you.

WATCH WHAT YOU PACK. Never pack irreplaceable business documents or jewelry; carry them on the plane with you.

TAG YOUR BAGS. Make sure your luggage is tagged with your name, address and phone number, and that a tag of some kind is also placed inside your bags in case the outer tag gets torn off. You can also tie a bright piece of ribbon or yarn on your suitcase handle so that you can easily identify your luggage from all the other pieces on the carrousel.

121

CALL AHEAD. Double-check by phone with the airlines to confirm that your departing plane will be leaving on time — before you leave for the airport. Make sure whoever is going to pick you up at the airport calls and checks with the airlines to also make sure that the flight is expected to arrive on time before they leave to go to the airport.

Making Meetings Count

When it comes to meetings, most of us behave as though we had never heard that time is money.
Michael LeBoeuf

Meetings can provide the setting for an exchange of brilliant ideas and the negotiation of important deals. Or they can be a major source of frustration, accomplishing nothing whatsoever and wasting everyone's time.

Effective meetings should lead to productivity and results — two of the byproducts of a streamlined life. Obviously, meetings with no apparent purpose should be eliminated. But for those meetings with a clear-cut purpose, often the outcome of the meeting is directly tied to how the meeting is set up and run in the first place. Some simple changes in how and when you have meetings could make all your meetings count:

HAVE AN AGENDA. Don't call a meeting if you can avoid it, but if you must, set an agenda and stick to it at all costs.

DEFINE THE OBJECTIVE. Don't call a meeting unless you have the objective clearly defined and written down. Keep the meeting on track so that the objective of the meeting can be achieved.

TIMING IS EVERYTHING. Have meetings either first thing in the morning, when everyone is anxious to get on with their day, or at the end of the day, when everyone is anxious to leave. Meetings are less likely to drag on unnecessarily at these times.

THINK BEFORE YOU SPEAK. If you are a participant in a meeting, you can issue diplomatic (and not so diplomatic) reminders when things get off the track. When conversation begins to wander, ask, "Could we get back to the issue at hand, please?" When a new subject is introduced, don't be afraid to point out, "That is not on the agenda—let's table it for our next meeting." And time warnings are always good; "We don't have much time, can we move on?" or "We're almost out of time, can we wrap this up?" are good reminders, along with looking conspicuously at your watch during the meeting.

START ON TIME. Don't wait for anyone. And don't review material that's already been covered for latecomers. (If you want to make sure that people arrive at meetings on time, make the last person who arrives take minutes.)

LOCK THE DOOR. To avoid interruptions and to eliminate the disruption of latecomers' arrivals, lock the door as soon as the meeting starts and ignore any knocks that occur during the meeting.

DON'T SERVE FOOD. Don't serve refreshments at meetings unless you must. Eating is distracting.

CHECK, PLEASE. If you must meet in a restaurant, ask for the check when the waiter brings the food so you won't have to chase it and waste time later.

DO BREAKFAST RATHER THAN LUNCH. Breakfast meetings generally find the participants more alert than they would be at lunch, and since they are anxious to get on with their day, they won't drag out the meeting any longer than necessary. Lunch meetings are at the mercy of service—which is usually slower than the service at breakfast — and people often have a drink or two before they eat. If you must meet for lunch try booking the reservation early, before the lunch rush (around 11:30 A.M.) or late, after the lunch rush (after 1:00 P.M.).

CUT THE BULL. Don't let meetings turn into a bull session or a coffee klatch. Stick to the agenda; socializing can be done *after* the meeting.

DON'T GET STUCK IN THE DISCUSSION STAGE. Make sure all your meetings move briskly toward the *do* stage. Insist on results. A meeting should result in decisions at the very least, and possibly tasks assigned. To ensure that those results don't dissipate after the meeting, be sure to summarize the decisions made, the tasks assigned and direction developed in writing. Send copies to those who attended the meeting, along with anyone else who might need or benefit from the information.

LIMIT COMMITTEES. Don't let committees operate forever. They should be established for a specific purpose only, and the deadline for action and results (and therefore, the elimination of the committee itself) should be established early on.

SET QUITTING TIME IN ADVANCE. Let everyone know what time the meeting will be over. Then make sure you end it on time. If you want to end an impromptu meeting, stand up. It's a hint that's hard to miss.

Remember, special occasions need not throw you off your streamlined track. Simply adjust your attitude, prioritize and plan, eliminate, organize, and systemize the requirements and components of those special occasions, and they can be as streamlined as the rest of your days.

A Final Word About Staying Streamlined

With only plain rice to eat,
with only water to drink,
and with only an arm
for a pillow,
I am still content.
Confucious

Streamlining your life might lead to a feeling of "resurrection." Leslie Martin of Cupertino, California, sees it that way, as she methodically takes stock on a yearly basis with these methods and quiet thoughts:

Resurrection
by Leslie K. Martin

Last year I didn't lose the extra thirty pounds. I didn't make a million dollars. I didn't find the love of my life. My tennis game still lacks a serve.

Recently, I initiated my annual purging. It's a ceremony I go through every year at this time. It's a quiet one, without pomp and circumstance. No one else knows of it or takes part in it. I never know exactly when I'll start—it's not something that gets logged on a calendar. Maybe it's the clearing of the smog and the literal breath of fresh air, maybe the transformation in colors and temperature makes me restless. But generally, somewhere after Halloween, when the weather changes and the air turns crisp and clear—you know, the kind of day that makes it hard to breathe but easy to think—I'll step outside and see that cobalt blue sky and know it's time to start.

I turn on a backdrop of quiet, moving jazz or maybe some rhythm and blues, and begin. It's a slow process because a lot of it is emotional. I often think how crazy it is to start something so large and momentous. But I take it at my own pace and fit it into my daily business, and work through the paces of it until the end of the year, when it rolls of its own weight, to completion.

What it is, is a methodical cleansing of every aspect of my life. I start with the physical manifestations of my existence. Every closet door is opened and every last object tucked into dark corners is brought into the light for examination and as- sessed for value. I don't mean tangible value. I mean whether it still has a place in my life or not. Anything not referenced or used in the past year is placed on a *For Sale* list or given away to brighten the Christmas of someone less fortunate. There are some objects whose value is difficult to assess. An item I have never used, but that I love because a dear friend gave it to me; an item I loved too much and have worn beyond recognition. If the time is right, I can throw the item away and it will retain the memory and the feelings it gave me. Once the chaos of all the physical items has been settled, the real work begins.

In my den there is a drawer that contains a year of my life. It is filled with the postcards, letters and photographs of all who cared enough to correspond in the past twelve months. It also contains copies of some letters that I sent to others—communi- cation efforts that were unusually important to me. It also has sporadic journal notes from days when something in my life needed to be set down in black and white.

I read every word I find in that drawer. Slowly, friends not heard from in recent days appear next to me. The impact of a personality hits full force after reading several of their letters at a time—it's as though they're reading them to me—I hear their phrases and intonations. Old love letters bring smiles and tears. All the relationships that have continued, changed, grown or been lost are refound.

When we take time to move carefully and deeply into the memories and events of our lives, interesting things happen. A picture of who and what we are at this moment in time begins to emerge. From longtime friends' letters we get a reading of our foibles; we see instances in which we weren't as good or as smart or as caring as we might have been. We also see why our friends respect and admire us, why they value our friendship

Along the way somewhere, there is a catharsis of spirit. It becomes clear which emotions and ties it is time to let go of, what can be forgiven, completed and released. It also becomes clear which relationships and endeavors are healthy and should be tended and nurtured. There is a sense of continuity of life as it ebbs and flows, and of the need to maintain a balance through the changes. And there is the revelation that whether or not we have patience, time is patient and provides us with the matrix in which we have the power to change whatever we like in order to make our lives better.

This year, I might lose the extra thirty pounds, I might make a million dollars. I might find the love of my life. And who knows, my tennis game could even grow a serve!

© 1990 Leslie K. Martin.

It is all to easy to fall off the streamlined wagon. Getting sidetracked by life's daily details and demands can mean that your attitude slips, you forget to prioritize, somehow you start accumulating more than you need and don't eliminate what you don't need — and you fall into the chasm of disorganization, with any systems you had in place gradually disintegrating as the final coup de grâce.

The best way to combat this possibility is to remind yourself every day *why* you want, and need, a streamlined life — what it really means to you. With your reason firmly fixed in your mind, quickly review the Five-Point Streamlining Plan, and commit yourself to applying at least two of the principles each day.

Remember this: *If you are willing, you can make it happen.*

Whatever you do, and however you do it, do it daily. Be persistent. The power of persistence is unlimited. Calvin Coolidge said it best:

Nothing in this world can take the place of persistence. Talent will not; nothing is more common than unsuccessful men with talent. Genius will not; unrewarded genius is almost a proverb. Education will not; the

Index

About the Author

Organization and time management consultant Stephanie Culp is the author of several books, including *How to Get Organized When You Don't Have the Time*, *How to Conquer Clutter*, and *Organized Closets and Storage*. She is the owner of the organization and management consulting firm THE ORGANIZATION. Her firm designs and implements systems and establishes procedures to help businesses and people get, and stay, organized.

As a national speaker and seminar leader, she has helped thousands of people help themselves get organized. She is also the publisher of *Organizing News*, a newsletter that features organizing and management tips and techniques for personal and professional lifestyles. Her articles have also appeared in several national publications, and she is a contributor to the *Los Angeles Times*.

Culp served as a delegate to the White House Conference on Small Business and she is a founding member and past President of the National Association of Professional Organizers, where she was the recipient of an award for her outstanding contribution to the field of organizing.

Stephanie Culp designs and implements systems and establishes procedures to help businesses and people get, and stay, organized. If you, your group, or company would like to have Stephanie help you get organized or serve as a speaker or trainer, you may contact her directly at:

Stephanie Culp
THE ORGANIZATION
P.O. Box 108
Oconomowoc, WI 53066

(414)567-9035

world is full of educated derelicts. Persistence and determination alone are omnipotent. The slogan, "press on" has solved, and will always solve, the problems of the human race.

Your life can be as simple and as streamlined as you are willing to let it be. It can stay as simple and as streamlined as you are committed to making it be.

It is entirely up to you.